# RETURN OF THE QUEENS

BY INE VERLINDEN

Thanks to all who have, do and will touch my heart and soul

# CONTENT

INTRODUCTION                                                          11

CHAPTER 1: WESTERN HIS-STORY AND FEMININE SYMBOLISM                   15
**Femininity and masculinity**                                       18
  Imbalance                                                          18
  Balance                                                            21
**The divine symbol of femininity**                                  24
  Reintroduction for our children                                    24
  Reintroduction for society                                         26
**The earth symbol of femininity**                                   28
  Her story and steps                                                29
  The nous                                                           33
**The unwritten part of femininity**                                 37
  Nature's wisdom                                                    37
  Truth is found within                                              39
**The consequences for Western women, and men**                      42
  The souls of systems                                               42
  Untapped power                                                     44
  Lost feelings, lost balance                                        47
  Journeying back and further                                        49

CHAPTER 2: BODYFULNESS                                                51

**Feeling consciousness**                                            55
  Sensuality                                                         55
  Grounding in your body                                             58
  Freedom in stillness                                               60
**E-motions**                                                        64
  Messengers of love                                                 64
  Shining mirrors and projections                                    68
  Power and powerlessness                                            73
  Forgiving history                                                  78
  Bonding joyfully                                                   81
**Collective unconsciousness**                                       87
  Uncherished natural principles                                     87
  Hidden feminine beauty                                             90
**Balancing relaxation and tension**                                 93
  A tensed culture                                                   93
  An enriching culture                                               95
  Opening and releasing                                              98

**The cycles of nature**     102
  Manufactured cycles     102
  Natural cycles     105
  The power of creation     108
**Our core**     112
  Life and death     113
  Surrendering to cosmic love     119

CHAPTER 3. BODY FOOD     123

**Physical food**     126
  Habits and beliefs     126
  Sustainable ways     130
**Energy in motion food**     135
  Digesting personal messages     136
  Happy food     140
  Levels of relationship     142
  True colours     144
**Soul food**     147
  A bridge     147
  For eternity     149
  Passionate living     152
  With open heart     155
**Nature's food**     158
  Pure consciousness     158
  Tuning in again     160
**Cosmic food**     165
  Left and right together     166
  Abundance     168
  Exquisite heritage     170
  Receptivity     173
**Tantric food**     178
  Daring to love well     178
  Uniting poles     185
  Opening up fully     189
  Sharing in love     191
  Making rainbows, a way of lovemaking     194

BIBLIOGRAPHY     199

*If there is to be peace in the world,*
*There must be peace in the nations.*
*If there is to be peace in the nations,*
*There must be peace in the cities.*
*If there is to be peace in the cities,*
*There must be peace between neighbours.*
*If there is to be peace between neighbours,*
*There must be peace in the home*
*If there is to be peace in the home,*
*There must be peace in the heart.*

Lao Tse

# Introduction

Knowledge versus wisdom, how intelligent am I versus how am I intelligent? A world of difference, and yet so complementary. At the age of twenty-five I felt I had grasped enough knowledge, I could see the patterns in the environment I was living in and was longing to be surprised again. I wanted to be touched by wonder again and was deeply attracted to the mysteriousness of life. And so I left the environment of Western intellectual thinking I knew so well and walked into a new world, to discover the realm of wisdom. In that world, I gradually came to realize my own intelligence, a deeply feminine intelligence. One that every woman carries deep down in her core. To fully put that intelligence into practice, it was necessary to reach osmosis between my left and right brain hemisphere, between a critical spirit and being open, between the management of my knowledge and the discovery of the unknown, allowing two worlds to collide, at every step.

Being an intelligent woman with a fascinating career, I chose to step back from the masculine driven business world for a while to focus on the development of my femininity and bring it more into my life and career. With this work, I want to share the feminine intelligence I rediscovered, an intelligence that brings back the stability, grounding and joy of every woman and man. A queen is a woman who has mastered these qualities, she is the woman who captures the whole energy of this book. She holds the power, all wisdom and knowledge of feminine leadership and knows how to connect to masculine leadership, inside and outside, as that is her role. She is not about female leadership, but about bringing her very own essence to the table, making it unite with all seated there with her.

Since I was a child I have always been curious, observant and looking for the deeper meaning of things. It was the best attitude for easy and fun learning, and I loved it. So I became a researcher. Initially in the sciences of business and innovation, and when I grew older this broadened into exploring new realms of human capacity, for lasting innovation happens at the personal level. For researching this grand theme of the essence of life, on how to live and care for life as a woman, my Western scientific path proved to be in dire need of a sparring partner to find essential answers and guidance. So I looked for a path that would allow me to go beyond my controlled comfort zone, but still feel welcome and safe in case I stumbled upon findings that would completely rock my world. And thus my research field broadened to other unknown, but deeply interesting territories. I researched Eastern and Western mystic schools such as the Christian, Buddhist, Taoist, Vedic, Yogic, Tantric, Sufi and Native American teachings, quantum sciences and other research fields on the vanguard of human consciousness, unconsciousness and development. I set out to connect these different worlds, where Eastern viewpoints meet Western ones, combining the best of both worlds. I questioned everything I believed to be true about the way we look at the world in the West, about the systems and concepts our society is built upon, about the way we relate to one another, about the way we experience love and union, or the lack thereof. It all added up to questioning everything I was taught about being a woman in this world. I was stretched very, very profoundly. Needless to say, the findings and guidance on womanhood in this book will evolve in their time too. They are to be adapted to every specific situation. Quantum science has beautifully shown how information is formed by the observer, being you as a reader. You will decide what to do with this information, and what to connect to the existing connections inside your system, active ones and latent, dormant ones.

These writings come from the connections my heart, gut and brain have made from all the information I gathered throughout the years. I am aware that my neural plasticity is in full force, that it is creating new connections all the time. We have billions of neurons in our brain and hence an astounding amount of possible connections. Our unconsciousness even holds ten billion times more information than our waking consciousness. It is our unconsciousness that processes every piece of information that enters our system but does not make it to our waking consciousness. And so much information stays hidden all too often, especially in a culture that has little time. However, by picking up this book your unconsciousness shows it is ready to be triggered into your consciousness and become the pure version of your expression of feminine intelligence again. Just like me, you must have been yearning to lift yourself and your world out of patriarchal culture, into a balanced world where feminine and masculine support and feed each other, where you as a woman are empowered to create and develop our human society. Being of the same species, as women, we hold similar patterns, similar wiring, the same history. It is time for our femininity, our deep joy and stability, to step up with the back-up of our refreshed masculinity, each in its unique way. When a group of women is ready to bring their shadow, their unconscious and hidden parts into consciousness again, that is the time women go from being tough to being truly strong, and gentle and passionate at the same time. That is the time of the Return of the Queens.

This is a book of personal inspirational thoughts. My own journey led me to reflect upon our society too. You will find both the personal and societal perspectives, in this book. You can read it from where I started my pilgrimage, full of questions, building up to making the circle whole arriving at my destination, having found many answers, or you can pick a topic here or there. Read it to your liking. I hope that the neurons and every cell I touch upon in your head and your body, may open and inspire your mind, body and your heart and its secret chamber. As that is the gift I wish to give you and the world with these writings, you as a unique symbol of true womanhood and your open secret chambers for you and all to enjoy.

*'She said... I am older than the mountains and the seas, older even than the stars; yet I am yours; and you are mine forever: and I shall make thee beautiful in mine eyes...',* written on a painting I received from my first partner who told me the Koran says that women already walk on heaven from their birth...

# CHAPTER I

# Western his-story and feminine symbolism

All wisdom schools and religions are about creating heaven on earth, whether they are practiced in the north, the south, the east or the west. They may emphasize other accents, they may even each have their strengths and their weaknesses, but in their core, they all share the universal value of creating heaven on earth.

What I noticed however when I was following the Western example of what it was to be a successful grown-up woman, I was in no means capable of creating that heaven on earth. I looked for role models, in my surroundings, in the whole of society, even in movies, but I could not find any woman having realized heaven on earth. Why was that, what happened that there were no women for me to look up to so I could grow into the radiant energy of what it is to be a woman?

Being the researcher that I am, I started to explore and look into it deeper and deeper. Since I really needed an example of true feminine beauty, I went on a pilgrimage to the Basilica of the Holy Mary Magdalene in France together with a female friend. From there on I started to trace the feminine symbolism engrained in my cells.

I quickly learned that separation appeared to be very characteristic to our modern Western cultural roots. And as such along the millennia a separation, a dichotomy had also taken place in the portrayal of the feminine. In Western culture it became Mother Mary and Mary Magdalene together that shaped the symbolism of the feminine. Mother Mary represents the divine aspect of femininity, the soft, the sweet, pure and the nurturing aspect. Mary Magdalene represents the earthy aspect of femininity, the physical, the sexual and the intuitive wise aspect.

Our Western collective image of femininity, our individual and collective experience of femininity, both as a man or a woman, is based upon the portrayal of these two mythic women, whether you are religious or not. Cultural roots go deep. They influence our upbringing, our view of the world, the way we relate to all in that world and our experience of the universe. Our mirror cells are coloured by our roots, by our myths that teach about life and how to live it. Mother Mary and Mary Magdalene act as mirrors for every woman in the West, for any woman even, as Western culture has found its way into practically every modern day culture, abundantly portrayed on television, movies and every media around.

Should both these women have been honoured equally, every woman would have had a beautifully balanced image to reflect upon. But when one is seen as holy and the other as a sinner, there is no possibility whatsoever as a woman to feel completely whole, or to ground gorgeous divine femininity. You will never be capable of respecting yourself completely if one part of you is not considered worthy to be here, that it can only be good through repentance. And this is felt by both men and women. Although women are the first bearers of feminine energy, they are the embodiment of this energy, men carry feminine energy as well. Moreover, every man comes from a woman and needs a well-developed feminine counterpart to channel his energy properly, hence he experiences this lack of wholeness too.

These two aspects of the feminine, the divine and the earthy, have only been placed in a dual role in patriarchal societies. In reality they belong together. Together they form a whole, the different facets of the feminine energy. It is from this whole energy that we can all embody and create heaven on earth, both individually and collectively. To experience the advantages of this wholeness, the joy and peace of it in our daily lives, we need to make a shift from separation to connection, from choosing either heaven or earth, to choosing both and connecting them here and now in our daily lives.

# Femininity and masculinity

Before going into the two aspects of femininity in Western history, we should look one step further down the line, the Western portrayal of femininity in relation to masculinity. I want to emphasize that this is not just about men and women, but about yin and yang energies. This book is not about feminism, in the sense that it is only about women. Yin, the feminine energy, is energy directed inwards. It is passive and cool. Yang, the masculine energy, is directed outwards and is active and warm. They are each other's poles, invisible versus visible, inductive versus deductive, union versus separation, matter versus energy. Both men and women carry both. Patriarchal consciousness sees either one or the other, it divides and consequently is hierarchical in nature. There is no problem with a natural hierarchy, as long as it considers the base as important as the top, the east as important as the west, the internal as vital as the external. It is essential that you can grasp it is about both, not one or the other. Like the yin yang symbol, together both parts create the circle. It is utterly essential to understand that it is all about the circle. With yang characteristics you give form to life, without them, all stays too ethereal. But this yang power is to be guided by the feminine part.

## Imbalance

When hierarchy is based upon an imbalance, where the top is more valuable than the base, it creates constant imbalance and stress. The core imbalance that societies and their corresponding thinking and systems hold, is that the masculine is more valuable than the feminine. You can see it in its physical form, by men acting superior to women or holding more elite jobs. In Europe in 2015, men are still paid more than women for the same job. In the US the separation and segregation on a physical level go even further, an African American woman earns less than a Caucasian woman. And in Belgium, the country of my birth, a country with one of the highest standards of living, the group most overrepresented in poverty statistics are single mothers. To me such lack of support does not represent a highly developed culture.

If you go a step further, you also encounter the imbalance in the form of qualities. In Western society we can easily see that rational intelligence has dominated feeling intelligence. When the circle is not honoured, the masculine can only see separate parts, it focuses on doing, doing and doing some more. You can see it in the paradigm of development, cold, calculated, cybernetic thinking that conquers, builds and uses without any feeling to it. All the emotional aspects, the feminine ones, both earthy and divine, are neglected in our society and therefore in every individual that brings these qualities to the table to contribute to the balance. The soft, the sweet, the nurturing, the physical, the sexual, the intuitively wise and the energetic represent no honour in high business and political mandates. And when I talk about the sexual, I talk about how to use sexual energy as a creative force to transmute lower energies into higher frequencies on the one hand and how to create a sacred third from two individual energies on the other. When sexuality comes into play in Western society it is most often more about release and dominance, staying in the lower frequencies. In these high mandates, few are allowed to use their intuition, everything needs to be calculated, with calculations based on past events and numbers, with no room for uncertainties. We live in a society that has created certainty where actually there is none, or at least not in the way it is presented. And why is it that a woman receives money for nurturing a company, but does not receive any financial gain or support for nurturing her own children to become contributing citizens? How is it that a CEO of a company that only upholds the interests of shareholders, earns tons of money for a job that requires coldhearted rational decision making without taking into account the cost of externalities, which are the costs the damaging load a company puts on society? Several years ago MIT published an article where it stated that seven out of ten CEO's have the same psychological mindset as psychopaths. Would it not be wiser to pay a CEO more when he has a high emotional intelligence as well as his or her rational intelligence? Would it not be wiser to put truly highly skilled people, who have the capacity to connect all the dots, in high mandates? People who understand the African Ubuntu? Would putting femininity back on the agenda, next to masculinity, not create more sustainable actions that better the whole, so we can all be closer to heaven on earth? Where each man is a true king again and each woman a true queen?

All this confusion is tangible in families too. Sometimes it is almost as if men and women have changed places. The women carry a very hard energy and the men are too soft for their masculinity to stand. This finds its cause early on in life. The girls have no women to identify with, who model balanced energies. They look for what is omnipresent, women following a dominant masculine principle. 'This creates women with masculine shields', like David Deida describes, 'hence they identify with masculine powers, with intellect', which is not the same as intelligence, 'or they identify with external beauty', sometimes with both.

And since men have no balanced role models either, 'men on their part often choose a feminine shield, being utterly social and looking for inner connections through alcohol or drugs', a make-believe emotional world. Neither one knows how to embody femininity or masculinity, let alone combine both within and manifest both externally. Needless to say true loving relationships and truly astounding collaborations seem as if they are from another world.

# Balance

In early Christianity the balance between masculinity and femininity was represented by Jesus and his consort Mary Magdalene. Jesus is the embodiment of perfected masculinity, he represents the outer, active, positive aspect of the oneness, completed consciousness, also called the Christ consciousness. Mary represents the silent, esoteric, inner, intuitive part of this consciousness, the feminine aspect. This interpretation requires an open perception, as active and positive should be understood in the broad sense. The feminine is also active, but her actions lie in the inner realm of reality. Negative should not be understood as not good, but as one pole in the electrical flow. Like the night that is not worse than the day, they just have their own characteristics that complement each other. Together they are one. Their balance brings peace.

According to Eastern energy teachings this unity happens in the sub-chakras somachakra and kameshvara chakra, which lie in between the sixth and seventh chakra. Chakras are energy focal points in our body, which physically correspond to our nervous centers or plexus. We have three lower and three higher chakras that are connected through the heart chakra. The more these centers of consciousness are activated, the more access you have to universal intelligence. When you can align the first chakra, where Shakti the feminine resides, with your highest chakra, where Shiva the masculine resides, you reach enlightenment. In Christianity this is portrayed by the halo that surrounds the head of saints. At this high level of development, when the sixth chakra is mastered, the duality of Shiva and Shakti, male and female, solar and lunar ceases to exist. Masculine and feminine energies are finally balanced in the kameshvara chakra. This is the union of the three aspects of consciousness, knowing, feeling and doing, as well as the union of truth, beauty and goodness.

This symbolism is portrayed in today's movies too. Movies that refer to tribal culture, like Avatar for example, illustrate the woman, the feminine, as the spiritual leader and the man, the masculine, as the communal leader. The inner versus the outer leadership, together forming strong leadership for a prosperous and peaceful society. It signifies the union of the two brain hemispheres. The inner meeting of the masculine and the feminine, the perfect harmony between left and right, absolute balance between logical and illogical, between Plato and Aristotle, creating a mystic union, the melting of the polar opposites. Knowing when to emphasize which power is therefore a trait of excelled leadership.

In the old days, those who had access to education received a royal priestly training. The women were taught by priestesses and the men by initiated priests. Both were taught to use their natural energies and powers. A future king was trained to learn to use his power. He was trained not abuse it, or better said, not to become abused by it, as power comes with a lot of responsibility. Not all are capable to handling it. It was of the highest importance that a king would always live for and lead the people. Being corrupted by power was not a royal quality. However, being an honourable king required much spiritual training. Therefore kings were supported, guided and advised by spiritually developed men and women, people who knew and practiced the wisdom of the universal laws. Olivier Chambon, a doctor psychiatrist, put this beautifully, 'People who know to tap into and use universal powers, who have experienced the divine can never again be in love with power, for they have learned the power of love'. As such, a queen had to be an initiate as well. She had to create a unified field with her husband, so he could accomplish conveying unified energies. When Mayan and Mongolian prophecies spoke about a changing 5400 year cycle in 2010 -a change from the 'Era of Man' to the 'Era of Woman'- I see it as men being part of wo-men. Together they create this unity again, worthy, like kings and queens. As author and entrepreneur Ayman Sawaf said, 'Beauty will yet again be the sum of peace and joy, serenity and exhilaration, inspiration and enchantment, wonder and majesty'. The feminine and masculine will once again be whole.

# The divine symbol of femininity

So to create heaven on earth once more, we need to take both aspects of femininity into account again. When you look at the divine aspect that Mother Mary represents, at first it may seem as though this soft, sweet and nurturing aspect has held its ground in our society. But when you dig a little deeper, it is not so. Although I am very grateful for the hard work generations before me have realized, there was no such thing as deeply soft and sweet living for me to be successful in outer society. When a society is built solely upon masculine principles, focus, specialization, hardness and action are key. Those who introduce the opposite find themselves not being part of the club. Hence, a lot of rejection and pain is experienced by those who cannot or do not want to fulfill or follow society's norm. And rejection and pain are not particularly soft and sweet feelings. When main bearers of femininity, responsible to manifest it into society, become weak, we feel a void. A void caused by lack of a supportive structure, a foundation for them, to bring their part into society. This lack of foundation for strong softness and sweetness most often starts after the age of 6. It leaves deep wounds that need time to heal.

## Reintroduction for our children

At one point in my investigation I checked with teenage students how they saw Mary, what qualities they attributed to her. I read the most beautiful things, 'She gives you inner power, she beams love and friendship, she makes you laugh, gives you hope, is always and unconditionally there for you and listens to you'. They described her as sensitive, warm, comforting, loyal, a quiet soul, patient, courageous, open, respectful, trustworthy, forgiving and non-judgmental. You could read that half of the group had portrayed their own mother. They were lucky to grow up with a woman that still had these qualities. One girl however stated that she was unearthly, so idealized that she was not real anymore and too difficult to mirror yourself against. What she picked up was that Mary's perfection was not natural, not of a human nature anymore. Indeed this type of distant perfection was a slow evolution since the 15$^{th}$ century. It became finalised in the encyclical of Pope Pius IX, which stated the Immaculate Conception on December 8$^{th}$ 1854, ridding her of any sexuality and engrained natural processes in popular culture.

When I asked the students whether they recognized these beautiful traits in their daily life, in their surroundings, all I got were sad and silent faces. When I say that the feeling of lacking a divine aspect most often starts at the age of 6, I refer to the Western schooling system. Action and performance start at elementary school, and tend to start even earlier in kindergarten. We have created an educational system that is solely focused on industrial production, a masculine contribution to our world that has not been balanced out yet. Luckily more and more feminine principles are finding their way in Western education. Scholars of positive psychology speak of the 21$^{st}$ century as the century of wellbeing. This is a perfectly logical step in our human evolution. When we evolve from evaluation to evolution there will be room for softness again. It is no longer only about hard numbers and work. The gentleness of flow can find its introduction again.

This means that the void will no longer be passed on from generation to generation. However, for the last generations, having been taught otherwise, this means releasing the hard and painful parts inside of themselves to make room for the soft and sweet again. Nurturing does not only mean giving clothes, shelter, food and schooling the brain. Nurturing also means giving love, warmth, support and room to develop. If our caretakers do not teach us how to do that, we are to be our own caregivers, letting go of the old to bring in the new. When you know your pain is the sum of the pain of all your ancestors, it can ache quite hard, to forgive and release both your own pain as well as the pain of many generations before you. But when you know you always have the strength to see you through everything that life brings you, you already know you are a marvelous human being. We live in challenging times, opening up, incorporating and stabilizing the feeling realm is quite a role. Fortunately, we are also the sum of the courage of our ancestral lineage. Whatever degree of pain you are to forgive and release, you receive an equal depth of joy, softness, sweetness, nurturing and power.

## Reintroduction for society

Mother Mary not only represents motherhood for our own children, but for the whole of society. Economics comes from the Greek word 'oikonomia', meaning 'management of the household, administration'. It indicates the 'rules of the house(hold)'. Our soft, sweet and nurturing capacity still holds much potential to grow. Whether we talk about our family home, country, continent or planet, the same basic rules apply. Work does not have to be hard and life does not have to be a struggle, but it is essential that softness is part of the equation. The roots and rules Mother Mary has in nature, have to find their way into daily life again. In later Christianity, however, this was viewed as a pagan character.

As such they rid her of this quality of natural healing and nurturing through nature. The snake that had always been a symbol of fertility, transformation and feminine power got altered to a symbol of venom in the renewed image of Mother Mary. Similarly, it was only in 367 AC that the New Testament as we know it was fashioned in its current form. It was Anthanasius, archbishop of Alexandria, who wrote in an Easter letter which writings belonged to the canon, what their reference texts were, and which were defined as divine. Wisdom teachings that once were open to the public, like some from the Gospel of Philippus, were soon considered to be heretic.

Self-care is another essential part of the equation. Women in particular were taught to put the needs of others before their own. I was literally taught to put myself in a subordinate role to save another, just like Mother Mary supposedly did. But how can you truly care for another if you do not even know how to care for yourself? Here again, you recognize a patriarchal view of care, the outer above the inner. The deepest care and love, however, come from within. The stronger you care for yourself, the stronger and wider your care will reach in the outside world. It is a teaching by example, just like Gandhi's quote, 'Be the change you want to see in the world'. Start with caring and loving your own small self first, and it will naturally expand further out into society. It requires standing your ground, no misplaced gentleness or insincere compassion, but truly loving care, which at one point will attract loving care of others.

On our way back from the pilgrimage, we found a beautiful example of this energy at the palace of Versailles in France. Versailles holds much universal symbolism. The sun represents the ultimate enlightenment, living from the soul. The shell stands for the journey of life. The stick and the serpent for Shiva and Shakti, the energy rising up along the spine. The lions, another sun sign, indicate strong leadership. You also find many fleur-de-lis, the triple flame representing the wisdom, love and power of God, another name for the primordial energy. Despite the symbolism being omnipresent, for Marie-Antoinette, queen to the French Sun King, the palace of Versailles held too much intrigue. In the 16th century patriarchal culture was full-on and the king was not powerful enough to connect to the universal energy the symbols represented and lead the people. This special lady stretched her role as queen as much as she could in her days, and in the back of the domain she created her own area to be able to live a warm, familiar life away from the court and its ways. There she could raise her children close to nature and could intimately meet the most gifted innovative minds of her time. Marie-Antoinette's domain looks like a beautiful little village, as from a fairytale, a symbol for 'la douceur de vivre', the sweet and softness of living.

# The earth symbol of femininity

From Mary Magdalene, the embodied symbolism of earth energy, we can learn what she represents in essence. Her name is a Hebrew transcription and means 'tower', a metaphor for the infinite. To truly grasp her fundamental nature we need to look at her from a new viewpoint. Instead of using the old common viewpoint of patriarchal consciousness where separation is key, we look at her from a consciousness of oneness, where feminine and masculine energies are balanced and unity is key. A viewpoint in which humanity, the earthy, is not seen as inferior to God, the Divine, but as a part of it, equal, yet with different skills. Together they create a new world.

## Her story and steps

This difference in viewpoint is shown beautifully in the Gospel of Mary. It describes the 10 Commandments, but in a very unusual manner. Where the popular version says, 'Thy shall not…', here it says, 'Love shall not…'. It silences you instantly.

The evolution of 'Thy shall not kill', to 'Love does not shout: murder, because this darkens the soul. How can we kill what we love?' holds such deep nobility. There is no longer a pointing finger that punishes and rewards, instead a gentle, loving support is offered, an invitation to open your heart to Love. It holds freedom and strength, intelligence and independence. Such writings come from 'an independent, intelligent, learned, passionate, unafraid, unconventional, open hearted spirit', like Nahmad and Bailey write, 'One that feels profoundly and is direct in words and deeds. They are perfect to guide you in living with an open heart and free Love on all levels, so you can truly grow into God's image'. When I say God, I know for many Westerners this carries a heavy load. Like I said earlier, roots grow deep. I slowly released the negative connotation by substituting the word God by Love in every ancient text I read. It works magnificently and brings you closer to the true meaning of what is taught. So when I talk about God, I am talking about a bigger reality, a source of life, how you name it will depend on how you were introduced to it, through religion, nature, spirituality, science or another form.

When we went on our pilgrimage to the Basilica of the Holy Mary Magdalene in Vézelay, I learned that she is the patron saint of the prisoners. Prisoners in the broad meaning of the word. Just like when ancient texts talk about helping the poor, they do not only speak about the material side of it but also the energetic side of it, thus also helping the poor of mind and spirit. In our day and era since Western society lost balance between the physical and the energetic, we became very poor in mind. Mary, as a disciple, was the first who was capable of bringing her seven demons, her seven deadly sins, her shadow, her darkness back into the light. Alas, many have interpreted the texts literally, whereas they are meant to be read symbolically. Darkness is the symbol for all unknown, unseen and repressed, for the inner world. Since these are feminine attributes, carried by men and women, in the stories, they are personified by women. The Christian tradition speaks of the seven cardinal sins, wrath, greed, sloth, pride, lust, envy and gluttony, which are nothing more than low vibrating emotions, destructive energies that require transformation into higher frequencies or life energies. Change always comes from within. Hence, it is important to understand that her repentance is a symbol for energetic transformation. Darkness is not to be feared but to be brought into the light for transformation. It is fertile soil.

Similarly, 'virgins' has the meaning of 'spiritually pure people', people who live in the highest consciousness of pure being. More so, some speak of wrong translations, which lead to 'unmarried' being translated as 'virgin'. Hence, it was never meant for women to be ashamed of their sexuality for eternity. It is not that our earthy aspects, our lower chakras and energies are bad, they just need to be balanced, integrated and infused by the heart and the higher realms too, not to be destructive but constructive. Epifanus writes in 'Curiosities about Mary' that Jesus initiated Mary on top of a mountain, showing her that physical intercourse is the earthy image of divine unity. In the Gospel of the Egyptians Jesus says, 'When you have thrown of your robe of shame and the two have become one, the masculine has become one with the feminine, so that there is no longer a masculine and a feminine… then you have gained true knowledge (gnosis)'. Heaven on earth. And in the Gospel of Thomas he says, 'I will lead her so that I make her masculine for also she will become a living spirit like you men. Because every woman that will master herself, will enter the Kingdom of Heavens'. Again, this needs to be interpreted symbolically, not literally, in which men are superior to women, but as the necessity to join masculine and feminine energies in one person.

When I was digging into Mary Magdalene's story I was surprised that I could hardly find any statues of her, until the nun with the shimmering eyes at the Basilica told us that she is represented in the light. It was not unintentionally that she was called 'the apostle of the apostles'. She truly mastered the teachings, unity of the masculine and the feminine in purity, in oneness. June 21$^{st}$, the summer solstice, when the sun reaches its highest peak, the Basilica is illuminated by natural sunlight in such a way that you see dots of light from the doors along the nave, representing her footsteps gently walking towards the chancel or apse, the sanctuary or vault or the semi-dome, where the illumination is the brightest. Her gospel teaches about the seven steps the spirit needs to take to return to heaven, to oneness and freedom.

Within each level there is a demonic side, a teacher and an examiner that will only allow the soul to follow its course when integrated the lesson of that specific sphere. We can compare these seven levels with the seven chakras in Hindu teachings, or the seven levels of the Kabala tree. Hindu culture also states that Shakti, the feminine power that lies dormant at the base of the spine, in our churches symbolized by the entrance doors, needs to be awakened. By bringing the energy up along the spine, the aisle, she meets with her Holy counterpart Shiva at the top of the head, the Coeur. It is a teaching that you can find in every religion. It touches upon the universal aspect bountiful in all religious and ancient texts. Teachings about universal energies are abound in the mystical counterpart of every religion. A sufi master is different from an imam, a cabbalist from a rabbi, a monk from a bishop. The first ones teach by experience, the others by knowledge, only showing the way. Surely, some combine them. With the internet these teachings are accessible to everyone who wants to learn, though it requires a critical mind and preferably also a mentor. I loved it when I saw a nun praying in the crypt, exactly in the same way meditation is done in Eastern teachings. Another simple example of what we have in common.

# The nous

Another fascinating and important part in Mary's Gospel writings, is the mentioning of the 'nous'. The nous implies a direct, intuitive appreciation of truth. We come to the truth not simply as the conclusion of a reasoned argument, but simply as something that is so. The nous is hence no rational concept. You need to experience it to truly grasp it. On page ten of the Gospel it reads, 'Where there is the nous, lies the treasure'. And on page eleven, 'The breath connects life-death-life in the center point that is the heart, called the noon of our being. This is where the nous lies'. The nous is seen as the part that can see the vision of Jesus, who symbolizes unified love. And it is exactly this that makes us complete humans. Complete humans live in union, they do not suffer from the void, and as such, by their nature, create heaven on earth. They know how to overcome their surroundings, they have the wisdom to stay in equanimity despite their environment, they have learned to live by their inner feelings instead of being dictated by outer events. Like page twelve states, 'Make thy soul loose from matter. As soon as the two are divided, the uplifting can begin. The breath supports the soul and gives life, it is this what makes you loose from matter. It is through the nous that we see, for it is the eye of the vision in the soul. And it is with the vision of the nous that we overcome the outer in our inner nature'. It is about bringing soul into matter, seeing how our inner state of being creates our outer world and transforms it from within.

Mary Magdalene wants to know how to attain that state to see the light, the consciousness that can experience the nous. An act inspired by this nous, is always right for you, for others and for the entire world. The strange thing however, is that once Jesus starts to explain how to get to experience the nous, four pages are missing. These instructions on how to be a complete human being, on how to experience Universal Energy or God, or True Love, or whatever name you give this energy, have gone astray.

When I was travelling, later on, I held my eyes and ears open to know more about the nous. I went to Greece, where the word originated from. But there I only received explanations related to intellect. No one could give me a convincing definition nor teach me about the spiritual aspect, or it was utterly complex. It had to do with a mental capacity but it was still explained from a rational point of view. Until one day, while on a plane to London, I met an elderly Greek man who gave me an explanation that got closer to what I intuitively felt was worthy of the word. He referred to an empathic intelligence, an intelligence on an energetic level. Although I did not yet feel that this explanation was complete, I did have an eureka moment. We had a beautiful conversation and dreamed what it would be like if children would be taught about the nous again at school, the true original version of course. What magic would be part of our lives once more if such a gift would again be accessible to all? In South Africa one night at a bonfire, I met an elderly man from the Western shores of the UK. Strangely enough he knew the word nous too, as a very old word for sure, one that was no longer in use. He too knew it from the rational point of view, but he knew it. And then some months later I watched an internet presentation on the educational role of myths, when I suddenly heard a lady saying: '... and when the deity was yielding his nous...' I was astounded to yet again hearing this word, again from yet another side of the world. In Hindu images some deities hold a nous, it is light emanating, the energetic ring some hold on their finger. In Christian images we know it as the halo that appears above a saint's head. In Hindu culture the golden circle of light is the symbol for consciousness, balance, concentration, harmonious movement and for dharma, which is the path that is uniquely yours and in alignment with your highest good offering worldly and heavenly delights and happiness.

Putting all the pieces of the puzzle together I now understand it as being in the presence of God. Feeling the energy where everything is born from and everything returns to. It is experiencing primordial power. It is returning the energy of your soul to its essence, to its heart. I have had moments in meditations where I could feel the universal void, or hear celestial music, and lucid dreams where my heart was touched by a universal eye. The tingles I felt that night were from another world. A world I believe is open to us all. A state of being that becomes our second nature again, if we are prepared to do the necessary and release old outdated conditionings so we can attain our original state again.

Although some of the teachings are lost in the Gospel of Mary, we know that meditation, breath and reflection in silence are some of our natural vehicles to get back to such consciousness. Some talk about the rainbow bridge, the mystical bridge between the mind and soul, brain and heart, where the nous is located. It has its access point in the heart chakra. It is there that self-consciousness turns into God consciousness, where mind and soul become one and unite in the Holy Marriage. In Vedantic literature this bridge is called the antahkaranah, the bridge between the higher and middle physical mind, between Buddhi and Manas. Mary Magdalene symbolizing the earthly aspect, shows us this connection and unification can be attained through our connection to nature as well. At one point in South Africa I was walking silently through the forest, in a meditative state. I felt my disconnection to nature and I cried, and cried. But suddenly my whole surrounding changed and took on a glimmering light. I instantly felt a wisdom flowing through me, a feeling of knowing and being connected to all in the forest. It was as if I was walking in a fairy tale forest, yet in the real world. That moment I experienced the nous profoundly, with my eyes open in waking consciousness. A consciousness that one day will become a non-stop state. We can all realize this groundedness in the divinity of nature again if we are open to it. It is humbling and magnifying at the same time, it is bliss.

On our pilgrimage we came across another woman, Marianne, carrying this strength. I was quite surprised that on a leaflet showing the French presidents, all men, the first image was the bust of a woman, Marianne, the figurehead of the French Revolution. On paintings you see her with an uncovered breast standing on the barricades for the people, leading the revolution, marching forward for a better life for all. It is unclear whether she truly lived or not, but it is great imagery showing the power of women and a balanced femininity. Many women have carried this powerful spirit, like the abolitionists who freed the slaves, the suffragettes who won women's voting rights and the feminists who created more equal opportunities for women and control over their own bodies. A spirit we are all to set free within ourselves to become truly free.

# The unwritten part of femininity

It is important to remember that only a small part of our history has been written down. This was mainly done by the conquerors. For the largest part of our written history we have been living in a patriarchal culture. In those days when some women did write down knowledge and wisdom, they used pseudonyms to sign their texts so that their voices would somehow be heard and not lost entirely.

## Nature's wisdom

There were many books that held old wisdom, often pagan in character, the wisdom of natural laws. The library of Alexandria was the most famous library in the Ancient World. Its collection held all the books that had been written up to that time. During the reign of the Roman emperor Caesar, it counted more than 700.000 volumes. During the war between the pagans and the Church in 391 AD, however, the Temple of Serapis that held the collection, was destroyed. All the books of the pre-Church era were burned. Rome is often seen as the base of Western civilization. Therefore it is important to bear in mind that Rome has not always been this version of Christianity, but carries older heathen roots, roots grown strong in nature.

This natural wisdom got forbidden more than once. In the Second Council of Constantinople, the 5th ecumenical council, organized by emperor Justinianus in 553, the teaching of reincarnation got officially outlawed. Reincarnation is a perfectly natural phenomenon you can witness in nature. Leaves on trees grow green, turn red and yellow and then they die. They fall on the ground, feed the soil and the roots to make the tree grow strong, making the natural cycle of life-death-life. This prohibition slowly created ignorance about the basics of life.

It reached a peak during the Inquisition. Many people know this period in history for witches being tortured and burnt. It ended in the middle of the 19th century, only five generations ago. Yet, these witches were not only women, but also men who lived by the old ways. These were wise people who lived close to nature. Unfortunately they were not understood by those in power at that moment. During the height of that system, in Spain alone, more than 6000 people were condemned to death and many more tortured. They died indirectly. Imagine what an amount of power and wisdom was swept away. And today you can see that many still treat nature in the same way, destroying it without dismay. Witches were the keepers of the natural and cosmic laws, they were our shamans, protectors of the sacredness of life. Shamanism is the oldest culture of a global nature, a global system that came into existence long before there was any external communication technology.

More of such important information on the cosmic and natural laws is kept hidden, even in more recent times. There is the story of Father Pellegrino Ernetti, an Italian Benedict priest, who was famous for his studies regarding the Bible and pre-polyphonic, pre-Christian music. In the sixties he invented a device, the Chronovisor, which demonstrated that visible wave lengths from the past could not be destroyed, that they would not disappear. To prove this, he brought back a transcribed fragment from Thyestes, a play of about 200 BC that got lost. The device was confiscated by the Vatican, including the whole work of research by the scholars. In 1993 two surviving scientists from the project presented their findings before the Vatican, before four cardinals and a scientific committee. The information that was revealed then has never been shown and the Catholic Church remains quiet up until this day. Even if his work is debated, knowing the wisdom of ancient schools, Father Ernetti's work was on a good track.

# Truth is found within

Another aspect of this unwritten past are the sacred teachings of Jesus as followed by the Gnostics. They were mainly taught orally. They highly value the inner knowing, the gnosis. It comes from personally experiencing and living the relationship to the energy of God, instead of knowledge about God. The theologist Clemens of Alexandria, living in 2 AD, used the term 'gnostic' generally to describe 'a Christian who already had achieved a deep knowledge of the truth'. Their texts were considered secret, because the texts would only reveal their true meaning when one was capable to work with them in the inner realm. To know God intuitively meant having a deep knowledge of yourself at the same time, a knowing that could grow ever deeper. Hence the quote 'Know thyself' at the Temple of the Oracle of Delphi in Greece, and at the Outer Temples in Luxor, Egypt. The Inner Temples carry the proverb 'Man, know thyself ... and thou shalt know the gods' writes Ihsa Schwaller de Lubicz. It conveys that you will only know what you are ripe for. 'In 'Conversations with the Savior' the Lord said to a lady, 'Sister, nobody will be capable to ask for these sacred things, for only those who have something to place it within their hearts...'. As the saying goes, truth is found within. This view of overcoming ignorance, or shadows, to live in bliss, is also found in Buddhism, showing that a long time ago

Eastern and Western worldviews found a common ground. Professor Morton Smith of the University of Colombia proves that this same Clemens of Alexandria was quite good at the manipulation of old texts, and had the part of the marriage of Mary Magdalene and Jesus eradicated from the Gospel of Marcus.

Consequently it does not mean that when something is not written down, it did not happen, it is not vital or cannot be traced back. There are many archeological findings that point to very different information than our current knowing, information that we often cannot yet grasp with the average logic of our Western viewpoint. Pieces of information about life from pre-patriarchal times are scattered all over. With the amazing communication channel of the internet, material and cosmic knowledge that was once only accessible for the few, is now easily in reach for everyone. With every new communication channel, a new era starts. It requires a diligent mind, and our well trained logical skills are of an essential nature, but it also requires an open mind, a reflective and receptive mind. It entails a spirit that is prepared to walk paths yet unknown, roads that question your entire view of the world, that allow you to be shaken to the bone and give you the strength to stay up or stand up again in unknown territory where there seems to be no certainty, no logic, not even own created thoughts.

In our globalized world the rules of the game have changed. What once was successful to go about in life is suddenly not the best way forward anymore. Old norms are no longer enough to answer certain questions, old truths are even overthrown. Quantum physics is coming to terms with ancient old wisdoms, wisdoms that were handed down orally from one generation to the next, often only held in certain languages, of which we are each day losing one. Language is a very strong carrier of culture. When I was reading a book about proverbs from all over the world that in some way involved women, I was saddened to find out how many diminishing and aggressive sayings there are. Proverbs are a very subtle way of a cultural thinking, teaching and influencing our subconscious mind. We are now experiencing a paradigm shift, where dealing with uncertainty, nonlinear thought processes, intuition and collaborative power are indispensable new skills to guide us further along the path. These are feminine qualities that we are to uncover again, to build further upon a story long gone, a balance that once was and is waiting in our veins to be uncovered, lived and enjoyed again.

# The consequences for Western women, and men

When women are not taught to touch upon their core, they are incapable to find balance and peace within. Neither are they competent to fulfill their balancing social role. In a patriarchal culture, the feminine energy is undervalued. It is valued lower than the masculine energy, and hence, to be a fully valued member of society, women act according to the highly revered masculine values.

## The souls of systems

Much is being said about positive discrimination and creating more access for women to board rooms. Blatantly put, however, these women are often men in women's bodies. They are trained for the system they are working in, yet some succeed to alter it one step at a time. It is a system based upon 200-year-old mere masculine values. The foundations of our current Western economic and managerial organism are that old. I introduced a program in the management school where I was working, confronting the dean with that theme. I knew I was taking a long shot whether he would be open to it or not, as it would shake his whole world and career view. Although I had searched for writings from the hand of another academic dean to be able to address him in his own language, he was not able to be open and receive the information of true innovation. When your entire life and career is built upon a masculine dominating system, a system of control and false security, it requires a lot of courage, intelligence and flexibility to break through it and evolve to a higher level. It is like jumping into a dark hole, which I would advise against without support. But even in a dark hole you will reach ground one day.

This masculine dominated system is pervasive globally. Jobs that require mainly feminine skills, like education and healthcare, are highly underpaid. Contrary to the paychecks of managers, CEO's and shareholders in the private and public industry who, apart from some exceptions, still hold the voice of these old ways. Since most policy is still written by the ones who follow this old conduct, no real lasting change will be made. Real change and transformation is only possible when the people in the driving seat become deeply aware of the essence of their job, of the soul of their job. Creating a balance for themselves and society, a true balance that is only reachable when masculine and feminine energies are both incorporated and valued equally. When they become aware that their consciousness and soul, and the system they are working with, is in dire need of further evolution, than the transformation can manifest easily. When you understand that all is animated, that everything carries a vibration, including the systems that are set up, then you can understand that the system feeds you too, just like you feed the system. It is everywhere, but the easiest way to see it is with women in politics or with young people entering the workforce. You witness their change after a couple of years. Luckily, to a certain degree, programs on generational differences have found their way into business. But on energetic differences there is still a lot of consciousness to be developed to move into a 21$^{st}$ century way of being, thinking, and especially acting.

# Untapped power

The patriarchal system has fed women with fear. Fear of experiencing their feminine qualities, depriving them of making their livelihood in ways that are soul nourishing to them. And for men too. When I met an activist lady in South-Africa, I was surprised at how much anger she had inside. I quickly understood, however, that this was her driving energy. Her energy to break through the injustice and imbalance she had been confronted with in her life. And she had every right to express it. She knew how to do it in a sensible way and used her zeal to set up new programs in her community to ignite a shift to justice and balance. Hopefully more women learn to express this energy consciously, and observe its message. For if not, the energy of their anger will internalize and attack their inner system and their surroundings.

I myself, being a product of my culture and era, found much of that same anger. Anger against unconsciously being conditioned in believing that being a woman means being weak, weak in all domains, on the physical, emotional, mental and spiritual level. When I actually stepped away from living in a masculine energy, into living in my femininity, I was confronted with how profound belief systems influence the different layers of your life's experiences. It was not always easy. Under that built up anger was much blocked joy. It had turned into sadness. I had loved my work at the management schools, I worked and researched passionately, but when I made a change in my life to answer my soul's calling, to research in a feminine way too, from within, I too stumbled upon many cultural thinking patterns and beliefs that needed to be released to truly live in my feminine power. Like the older woman I had always used my zeal to realize change in my work domain. But I realized it was not about fighting or surviving in a masculine system, which brought me no joy ultimately. It was about loving and living in a system that honours femininity. A femininity that is balanced and fed by the masculine gains strength and feeds the masculine in her turn.

So a vast amount of joy and positive contributions is not being tapped into. It is true that women and the energies they represent have long been suppressed in more ways than one. Nonetheless it is up to the women themselves to reinitiate femininity into their lives again, at home and at work. It is definitely hard to come to terms with, but it is essential you allow whatever you observe to become stable and strong. You cannot expect a man to know what it is that a woman or society is lacking. Although more and more wise men are becoming aware of the lack, often they cannot find the exact words to express it. Since they often do not have fulfilled mothers and wives themselves, or fathers, it is not only the women that are feeling this imbalance, this lack of joy and bliss in their individual power. When talking to men in all levels of society, you can touch upon their sadness too. They too long deeply for a feminine touch that is nurturing and soft yet strong, to complement their masculinity. A femininity that is so strong that it can take them away from the twisted or weak masculinity into a deeply fulfilling and balanced masculinity. They too long for their origin, for true masculinity. They too want to feed women their strength, protection, love and honour. Do not believe that powerful men who have it all, according to current societal norms, are happy. On the contrary, they are often men who have lacked much love, more even than the average person. They have developed very tough compensation mechanisms to cope with this lack of love and bringing meaning to their lives. Luckily, as a natural law, everything looks for balance. And so men are stepping up to heal their part. Less and less wise and talented men keep developing mega office building facilities when there are so many vacant existing constructions. They no longer construct cities that are void of places for children to discover nature and its fauna and flora. They no longer contribute their talents to maintain a financial system that favors few and leaves many to struggle, nor to a labor system that forces a stranger to carry the responsibility for the upbringing of our children. These men do not put their focus on mere productivity any longer, neither do they consider wellbeing a second-hand commodity. They do not allow child soldiers and forced child labor to exist. No, on the contrary, these men, with their true and strong masculinity, protect. Wise women on their part are not solely focused on fashion and on physical appearance anymore. They are not maintaining a career according to masculine values, to build a so-called strong and independent self-image. No, these wise women honour the beauty of the fabric and make sure it is produced sustainably. They honour every body's figures and uniqueness and they create bioplastics and set up banks in countries where women need much support. Banks where only women can borrow money and women decide what the money is spent on, all to support of their society. Wise men and women do no longer contribute to a system that is deeply flawed. Instead they ask questions, as children do, and contemplate what it is that we have inherited from our elders. What is outdated and what is still supportive for all. What can we create based on the resources gained along the way. CEO's of the new economy fulfill their childhood dreams. They step into the feminine realm too. If necessary they feed themselves this exquisite beauty. Just like the kings in the old days did. And as such, they step forward as truly honourable men leading our society forward. Balanced men and women develop a new answer to life, a stable, sustainable, integrated answer. And luckily their numbers are growing each day.

## Lost feelings, lost balance

The problem is that when living in an imbalanced society, tensions are all-pervading and make the shift no easy job. Tensions misshape perceptions greatly and you must be very strong to break through long held boundaries. On average the system's flaws are not noticed. People have become so habituated to the tensions, they do not even question them anymore. Moreover, few people actually still feel the tensions because of desensitization. And so, on average, people make decisions that make it easy to ignore the tensions. Decisions that compensate the tensions, with all the consequences that entails. Of course it is an illusion to think that ignoring or compensating tensions means you do not feel them. There are many distractions that keep your attention from going within, that make you believe that you are happy. But just imagine what would happen if you would be on your own for 10 days without other company or external activities. Just try to sit on your own with your eyes closed and follow your thoughts. Try not to move and then feel your body. Observe how comfortable it is to sit with yourself for a couple of hours. Chances are that you will come across a lot of agitation and stress in body and mind, as that has become our society's norm. With some training you will fall into a serene silence where you are being carried away and your entire body becomes soft. Only when we can silence ourselves mentally and emotionally, can our body do what it needs to do. And this is the difficult part. If you cannot even sit comfortably with yourself and smile, how is somebody else going to do that for you?

Luckily again, you can bring back the smiles. Imagine a sick child that receives care. Just see what a big smile and glow comes upon his face when being cared for. Now give that to yourself too. If we take care of these neglected tensions, we make it easier, more fun and joyful to live together, under one roof, in the same street or country, on one planet.

It is essential to feel again. A feminine quality. So many women and men do not know how to feel anymore. Very often I get the strangest looks in my practice when I advise people to feel what happens in their body the days after a session. It was as if I was asking a fish to fly. Most often all attention is focused on the outside world, work, family and social life. When you look at our current societal outside world, the news is not really giving an incentive to start feeling again, as you will not particularly be feeling pleasant and comfortable feelings only. As long as you are not aware of the tensions you hold, you will keep scattering them all around, expecting others to clean up after you. Such behaviour has nothing to do with being a strong man or woman. There is no responsibility in this, no energy that corresponds to an adult. In Western society an adult is someone who reaches the age of 18 or 21. But someone can be 55 and still be a 5-year old when it comes to his or her emotional development. Emotions are energies in motion, e-motions, and when they are not guided in their current, tensions are built up and happiness and vitality are lost, and possibly much more. Neuro-anatomist Jill Bolte Taylor found that most emotions move through our body in 90 seconds or less, unless you decide to hold on to them. Meaning that we always have a choice to open or close ourselves to life. When we close ourselves too often too much tensions gets stored, a system failure will appear and one gets sick. The body will send an alarm that homeostasis, the balance between all systems, is no longer active. If wise, the alarm will be heard, felt, questioned and acted upon to reverse or alter the situation and reach homeostasis again. If not, a pill might be taken to suppress the uncomfortable alarm and the system will adapt itself to find a new balance. This new balance, however, has less and less to do with homeostasis. It is a balance that has shifted away from the original equilibrium point. And if that shift is stretched a little more every time, there will be a point of capsizing. One will get a burn-out, or if more intense, cancer cells transpiring to attain the original point of poise again. This naturally occurring flow does not only happen within our bodies. It happens within our families and systems too. The many collapses we see these days, are just a manifestation of a natural law. For sure these disequilibria do not only happen in Western culture, many have taken on a global nature.

## Journeying back and further

Being a young woman in a global society, I have been granted the opportunity to release myself from my patriarchal culture and have uplifted myself into a new one, a universal one. Our culture decides how we view the world. It is fundamental in everything we do, whether you are conscious about it or not. I was surprised to experience consciously how deeply culture is engrained in our system, even in our central nervous system. Although I was raised with the mind-set of women being strong, open and tolerant to other cultures, there was an undercurrent embedded with patriarchal cultural traits. When I started having experiences that did no longer fit my Western cultural paradigm, a paradigm intertwined with the centuries old culture of Newtonian science, I knew I was in for quite the ride. A ride of truly feeling that there might be other ways of seeing life, the earth and the universe. And luckily, changing your view of the world changes the world for you. Evolving your consciousness brings magic to life again, allowing you to experience it full on.

If we want to restore all systems again to their original equilibrium, we are to release the tensions and focus on wholeness, from the human body, over the economic system, to the planetary body. All cultures could be created in such a manner that they do not go against nature, but allow an open perception to trace and act upon the natural and universal laws again. It is a journey to our original state. More than progressing, we are to recover, restore and revive ourselves and nature in that which has been grossly overlaid. Now is the time to rediscover it. Die and be reborn. The women before me in the culture I have been brought up in have worked hard to open the path for me. They made it possible for me to have a higher freedom to develop myself, to travel the world and speak up with a truly universal voice, a true woman's voice. Not one that fights like a man but one that loves like a woman and protects like a man. Imagine the consequence of a past, present and future where his-story was, is and will be written jointly in honour and balance with her-story and with the story of the wise people. Imagine how you would see the world then...

*The path to inner harmony is natural and simple, in that it consists of asking 'Who am I?' and not giving up until you find an answer that puts you at peace, happy with who you are, and happy with the reflection that the outer world gives you.* - Deepak Chopra

CHAPTER 2

# Bodyfulness

For a long time women's self-images have been based on a masculine perspective, beauty being defined on the outside only. But to live in happiness and joy, a woman needs to live her self-image from a feminine perspective too. Beauty coming from within, beauty as energy, being relaxed, open and light, as that is a woman's wiring. A woman can only feel her own body as a heavenly thing on earth when it is sustained from her own perspective. It is essential to be honourable to your own ways, grounding your body in the earth, feeling it in every vein, loving it from deep within and as such enjoying the divinity of it.

Luckily, times are changing and with changing times come changing self-images. Research has amply shown that physical beauty and health have everything to do with the inner state of being. That an inner happiness, a being and acting true to your purpose, radiates throughout your body. It is all about energies, with love being the primordial energy. When you learn to open yourself to love and loving your true nature, it can permeate and flow through your entire body. It shines through your eyes, your smile and your skin. Everything starts to glimmer and glow naturally.

Your movements change and in that natural sway, in that power, others can experience and feel your deepest core, your authentic self.

When not all has been enveloped in love, not all cells will vibrate with love and vitality, nor will they vibrate your core. These cells might think they are not worthy of love, or only when they act in a certain manner, often different from what they came here to do. They might believe they are not allowed to be here, or only here to serve others instead of themselves too. Doctor Masuru Emoto's research showed beautifully how water crystals change shape depending on what type of messages they received. And Doctor Bruce Lipton's research found how cells deteriorated when placed in a petri dish with a negative culture, but also how easily they would regenerate when replaced in a different one with a positive culture. This field of research is called epigenetics. It deals with how our genetics is influenced by the dynamic between our inner and outer world. We are not a victim to our hereditary genetics, on the contrary, we are stronger and more powerful than we think. Our beliefs truly have big effects. When you imagine your body as being filled with crystals, like in Doctor Masuru Emoto's research, for them to be full, to be beaming, they have to be fed the proper food. False beliefs, hence, are not the best food. If the food has been more deteriorating than nurturing, the crystals will not shine as bright and their shapes will be all but exquisite. So we have to be conscious and alert to the words and stories we tell ourselves and others.

Research on consciousness shows that we actually create everything by our own mind. Everybody is creating another world with the several billion cells we each have to our availability. Every thought and every intention create chemical reactions, fire off neurons through and beyond the body. If you believe that you are capable of beating a cancer, you are, if you believe that you are not capable of beating a cancer, you will not beat it. If you believe you are beautiful, you will feel beautiful, if you believe you are ugly, you will feel ugly. If you want to see life as heaven on earth with a vast amount of possibilities, you are right that it exists, if you want to see life as hell on earth where you are stuck and have no way out, you are right, that exists too. This however, puts all the responsibility of the state of your life and body in your own hands. This can be quite harsh to swallow for some people, there is no pointing finger anymore. But no matter how harsh it may sound, it is simply the nature of consciousness as discovered by research. If you choose to look at it from a positive angle, it means you are capable of shaping everything in your world exactly the way you want it to be. It teaches you that you have a choice. You can look at the world through different lenses and each lens shows a different story and holds different consequences. It is like the saying 'Beauty is in the eye of the beholder' and the magnificence is that you can change your point of view at any moment. To live your dreams might require some intense consciousness work first but it is definitely doable. All energies, in all its polar forms, warm and cold, day and night, light and dark, hard and soft, creation and destruction, are all here for us to play with. It is up to each and every one of us to choose what and who to play with, and more importantly how to strike a dynamic balance.

It is our choice of play that decides what our individual and collective world will feel and look like. We are given the freedom of choice at every single moment. That is our main responsibility to ourselves and to others. As women it is our responsibility to tend to feminine energy first. Many people regard the word responsibility as having a heavy emotional load because it gets confused with duty, something that is not in balance with your rights. But if you take away that load and look at responsibility for what it truly is, you find that it is the gift of freedom to respond to life, both individually and collectively. It gives you the liberty to live your own authentic core and purpose fully, with your heart, body and soul completely engaged. Complete responsibility is therefore complete freedom. Try it for yourself. Go out and see through the lens where you are mastered by men or others. Look into yourself and into your surroundings and experience what you feel and see. And then change the lens. Let it now speak from the strong feminine side too, from your heroine or yourself. Listen to what it does to your story and how you feel now.

This feminine energy's voice speaks through feelings. It makes your body speak through sensations. That is why personal wellbeing should be your first priority, for it is a felt sensation. Before anything else, this is a child's main way of communication. Children pick up feelings easily, and whatever you wish to believe, you just cannot hide yours from them. We all hold much knowledge in our hearts, we sense intuitively, we know without knowing how, and we know by feeling. Walking through life in this digital and global era, you are bombarded with external information and stimulation that, consciously or unconsciously, heighten your inner sensations. They may overwhelm your body – your physical manifestation. But also your intuition, which is your soul's voice – your energetic manifestation. This may in turn overwhelm your heart and mind, making it difficult to live your authentic self. However, if you learn to live feminine energy, balance your body and intuition, you can live your unique dreams, your heaven on earth, and be the biggest and most beautiful present that you can give yourself and the world.

# Feeling consciousness

If we want to live in bodyfulness, we have to activate our feeling consciousness again. This means feeling our feelings and talking about feelings. For some it is like talking about flying like a bird at first. Like scientist Carlo Ventura says, 'We are used to describe what we see, not what we sense'. A culture of being in your head, of taking no importance on feelings and emotions has led to desensitization, to rushing from one place to another, to repressing and denying your body's alarm with pills. None of this will make your crystals be filled with radiant love. Our body holds our unconscious memories until they are consciously released. Illness is nothing more than a cue for transformation and sensing again.

## Sensuality

These days there is scientific proof of how our feelings influence our physicality. Doctor Candace Pert found how emotional molecules can be traced in the body. Yet the importance of our feeling consciousness was already known by ancient Egyptians and conveyed in 'the Eye of Ra', also called 'the Eye of Horus'. The Egyptian word for that symbol is 'Wadjet', which means 'God' or 'Goddess'. It is made up of six parts, each representing a different sense, touch, taste, hearing, higher thought as in intuition, sight and smell. The eye is a receptor of input, and so the Eye of Ra stands for these six doors through which we as humans receive data. All of this data input is considered to be the eye's food, thus the food of our brain, the food of God. When you know about the physical structure of the brain, you can see that the Eye of Ra is a physical copy of the inside of our brain. One part of it is the thalamus, the part of the human brain that translates all incoming signals from our senses. It decides which nerve impulses are sent through consciously and which ones are stored in our unconsciousness. This shows the importance of a developed feeling consciousness, of how and how much information your brain receives from your sensations.

The more you develop your feeling consciousness, the more you enjoy playing with your senses, the more sensuous you become as a woman. What are you tasting right now? Are you aware of any particular smells? How does your body feel, internally and externally? Can you feel the temperature or your clothes on your skin? Are you conscious of all your senses at once, experiencing the feelings within you and around you, your touch, tastes, sounds, intuitions, sights, smells? Can you expand your sense perception outward, until you can conceive feeling far away oceans and mountains? Of course this sensuality does not come from living in the fast lane, nor from superficial living. It is too much and too deep an information for that. For it to develop inside of you, you must go slow. You can start by eating slow, with all your senses, feeling, tasting, smelling, looking and listening while you are eating. Ancient mystics always knew the importance of living slow. Only then can you enter other dimensions, such as the realm of feeling and its senses. When there is no room for meditation in your life because you are going too fast, you can only perceive an ordinary reality, most people's experience. However, when you slow down, you can experience an expansion of your ability to perceive the physical and also the non-physical world through your senses. When you go slow and become silent within, you open up for the sacred in life, like seeing a tree breathe. Slowly you will get small signs of those short moments of connection that will increase your trust in the physical and non-physical world. Making more room every day for such experiences to become a peaceful, silent, strong and steady part of your life. As a woman it is essential you create moments to enter into this sacred solitude to connect to your senses, so you can relax and renew yourself. Feed your sense of touch with delicate fabrics and your taste with savory foods, pleasure your sense of hearing with pleasing and joyous sounds of music and laughter, feed your intuition by tuning in to ancient gods and sacred geometry, feed your sense of sight with looking at natural beauty, and your sense of smell with magnificent aromas of flowers.

Your senses are of high value as they give you direction in your life. They tell more about who you are, what suits you and what does not, what makes you happy and what does not. Not everybody gets happiness from the same things, just imagine a techie wizard and a flamboyant artistic painter. When you desire the perfect man for example, your feeling consciousness is telling you that you desire the feeling of loving and being loved. It is through our senses that we can perceive ourselves. They tell us so much about who we truly are, what our innate identity is, instead of artificially created identities. Imagine with every sense what it would be like to lose it. Imagine that you were blind, what would you miss? What do you need to experience a happy sight for you? Do you want to see happy people around you, or sad neurotic people, big steel constructions or big natural wonders, people dressed in black or people dressed in colour, or both? Which sounds make you happy and which ones make you sad? Do you hear enough laughter to feed your hearing? What tastes make your eyes widen? What scents touch your soul and which ones make you remember uncomfortable moments? How often do you touch another? Can you feel the sun or the wind on your skin? Did your mother touch you gently or was it a mere functional touch? How often do you intimately touch your partner? And if there is no partner do you feed your touch with a massage? The amount of information we gain via our feeling consciousness is so incredibly vast that it needs our attention. Every information gathering through sense is stored in our system. The happy gathering is fun and easy to experience, but when you push an unhappy gathering aside, it will sit where you stored it. It will crystallize into an emotion and tension until you give it its rightful attention and let it flow again. The more you learn to accept and live through the unpleasant things, the more they will help you grow. It is better to stop judging and let go of definitions that hold no universal truth.

## Grounding in your body

This feeling consciousness is active when we are born. As a baby, my twin brother and I were separated immediately after birth. We were placed in separate incubators for a month hardly being touched by our mother. This created a lot of trauma of separation and lack of support for me. And I kept playing out these imprints until I was ready to release them completely from my system. Since I was always wanting support, I created a compensation mechanism of offering non-stop support myself. Offering to others what I had lacked and deep down was still lacking. I had been aware of its influence on my life, but I unconsciously kept setting up conditions that would follow suit with my earliest memories of life, until I could completely release my body from the emotional molecules that had stored themselves very deep in my tissues and bones. In this post-industrial era, many babies experience this lack. There is too often no physical or emotional union between mother and child anymore. Breastfeeding is often not taken for what it truly is, a natural healing, bonding and protective system. Often an emotional bond is lacking between parents and child, as many women and men have not grown in their own emotional maturity. And on top of that, since the West, on average, holds hardly any notion of God, of an original universal force, there is no divine union between them either. When these feelings are not cared for, they are set to become emotions stuck in the body, until they are released and the experiences integrated. Emotions have to do with the past, whereas feelings are bodily sensations in the present moment. That is why the first have to do with pain and do not disappear on their own, and the latter have to do with purity, when they are being cared for in the present moment. It is up to you to decide which aspect you want more from in life.

Therefore it is important to be grounded in your body, to feel your body and its aliveness again. Become silent within. So silent that you can feel where it aches, where it feels neglected and where it feels strong and happy. Being grounded in your body means being aware of your body and its boundaries, being aware of the present, being aware that you are a person, an entity on your own, being aware that you are fed and carried by earth, that there is a downward energy that keeps you sticking to the ground, stable and strong. It signifies experiencing yourself as a whole. The earth is a highly receptive entity, it brings forth life, it takes in what is dead and transforms this into new life. Earth is nature, grounding is similar to corresponding to your own nature. Be connected to earth, to nature and your nature. In this way, grounding means to feel home, to be living somewhere nice and happy. When you reach happiness in your own nature, it becomes easy to connect as a human being with the bigger nature that is earth. Home then receives its meaning again on all levels, on the level of our body, our soul, our nature, our house, our earth. Like the Native Americans say, 'We are of the earth', and indeed biologically we are made up of the same minerals and masses that the earth is built of. It means being ok with all that life on earth entails, the positive and the negative. And, without judgment, we no longer see those as good or bad, but as relaxation versus tension, suffering versus enjoyment, creation versus destruction, life versus death, all being part of the same cycle of nature.

## Freedom in stillness

Our feeling consciousness is free of any judgment, it does not judge, it is our mind that does the judging. You can experience this in meditation. When I first got in contact with Vipassana meditation, I was taught to observe my inner sensations. I had to let them move without influencing them and let them do their thing. They all came at a certain moment and they would all go again at another. In this type of meditation retreat you are brought to your feeling consciousness while meditating ten hours a day. You are not allowed any contact with the outside world, so no writing, no eye contact, no singing, nothing, all to support you to make the journey within. The first time I was confronted with quite some aches and pains, and after a while I was able to just observe the pain. I was able to be fully present in the moment and accept them without resistance. First the physical pain showed and then the mental, it was very confronting to see my inner world, no one else to blame, no other things to focus my attention on but my own. You actually sit out the pain, if you just observe it without judging it, it truly fades. Similarly with the more fun sensations, again you only observe them, do not judge them or put a preference on them, as they will also just fade away. And by doing that, at one point, you can arrive in such a sweet vibe, all loving, gentle and harmonious. It was such a magnificent experience to see energy in my system in action like that.

When it was time for my second Vipassana retreat two years later, I saw it as an enormous gift of pure feeling for ten days. Ten whole days all being given to feel, feel and feel some more! I had no aches anymore whatsoever, it was easy to sit still for an entire hour and longer, all was soft and easy. The two years of going within, of self-inquiry and development had proven its effect. The surroundings of the meditation retreat of course, like the petri dish had a huge effect too. It had been snowing and all was white and pristine, everything was covered and silent, the only external action was the snow shimmering in the sunlight. It might have helped that the retreat were only women, where normally half of the space is for the men. It was wonderful to sit silently with yourself and 60 other women and feel and just be who you are.

A couple of days before that retreat, I had visited a physiotherapist who specialized in Chinese medicine. On the side he had mentioned that the Chinese had never cut open any bodies to develop their medicine, and during that retreat I could feel what the man had denoted. At one point, I had become so silent within that when I asked any of my organs of my body to show themselves, they started to pulse more vibrantly, as in saying, hello, here I am. I talked to each and every one of them, except one I found out later, I could even see my DNA and feel fluids. I could easily imagine how they mapped out all the nadis and meridians by this practice, how they could see and feel everything living as part of a whole. Later I read that once a quantum researcher, who had found new insights, got very upset with his findings as they shook up his entire mind, his findings were too mindboggling. He was then invited by an Eastern professor and was taught meditation. In the meditation the researcher had become capable of finding peace and understanding with his newfound land. Meditation helps you to tap into an intelligence that reaches much further than the mind can grasp. It activates your feeling intelligence which is highly rich and a vast source of healing, of innovation, in all, of wisdom that helps humanity move further and back to its core.

Meditation is going into stillness, into the here and now, which activates your self-healing mechanism. It is actively activating different brainwave frequencies, which naturally happen when we fall asleep and dream, but there are even deeper states than those. Brainwave frequencies are linked to certain physiological changes like your heart rate and breathing, but also to behaviors, feelings, and perceptions of reality. With meditation you go within and listen, do introspection, be active in the inner domain. Just like in daily life, you become quiet to listen to the one you are engaging with. Here it is not another's voice, but your own inner voice, sometimes there are even no words anymore, just pure energy. In this stillness you can track and trace any residues of emotional and physical points that need attention to clear the way for you to be fully present. Our bodies and minds are very responsive when we pay attention to them, as they prefer nothing else than to go back to the perfect balance, the place of living life without effort, open to the flow of life. This is what engaging in personal development is fundamentally about.

In stillness is where you can feel your creativity flow. Your own creativity, whatever form it takes, is like a channel within you that allows you to travel to sacred spaces within yourself. How many artists and scientists have told about being inspired from above, from something outside of them? This is when in stillness they touch upon extraordinary vibrations. When they are completely open and have surrendered to the process, they receive inspiration. Creativity truly is a door to the genius part of yourself and life. Can you imagine that at one point in ancient India the basis of its economy were artistic and crafted goods created in such creative union? Whatever the economy you live in, being able to return to silence and calmness, to a place of serene neutrality practically means that you can keep contact with your center, with the true and stable you, with your inner voice that is not over shouted by outer voices. It gives you a big advantage in a fast-paced world as it is in this place of silence that you can make conscious choices on how you want to relate to yourself and the outside world.

# E-motions

During the meditation retreat I learned that the physical painful and fun sensations I felt, found their origin in my mind, my thoughts and my emotions. These were energies manifested in the earth, in the physical, in my body. Physical manifestations I could decide on how to deal with energetically, without preference. Once I was able to let go my conditioned preference for the fun sensations and let go of the judgment of the painful ones, I reached a very tranquil state. Observation and curiosity with a smile, just like a child only now conscious.

## Messengers of love

When certain experiences and emotions are not dealt with because they are too harsh, too painful or too difficult to deal with at a certain point, they get locked in the body until a time when your system is ready to incorporate the e-motions and the learnings they hold. This is how we form and store tensions in the body. If not dealt with for too long they start to live on their own and turn into discomforts or further into disease. This is your body showing you your energetic unease with certain events in life on a physical level, your need for love for certain vibrations that are part of the rainbow.

To live in love requires first accepting and then releasing negative emotions and other conditionings that obscure your true nature. Emotions are information carriers, and it is all about how you deal with each type of information. Emotions do not work against you, they work for you.

Emotions are there for you to bring you to wholeness, to show you what you still have to work on, what pain has not been dealt with or what destructive cellular memories you still carry. If you learn to use them for what they exist, to show you whether you are living in alignment with your core, they become a source of much support and true allies in guiding you in life. Their purpose is in gaining true wisdom, for everyone. They truly talk a universal language, as there is no such thing as Christian anger or Islamic anger, anger is anger. The more you are in flow with your true inner nature, the less emotions will get stuck in your body and cause dis-ease. The more you judge, suppress or try to control your emotions however, the more pent up tensions you carry, finding its result in an unhealthy body or a very restricted controlled lifestyle. If you then have tensed people governing companies or countries, we all know where that leads.

However, since our culture has been focusing on the material much more than on the energetic, emotional intelligence is no part of our Western cultural heritage and we have to learn it, just like reading and writing. We are initially what they academically call an 'affectively neutral culture', one where feelings are carefully controlled and subdued and physicality is practically a taboo. It does not mean we do not feel, it simply means we are conventionally taught not to express emotions or feelings. To put it visually, I always find the corset the best example of our emotional heritage. Emotional literacy is no luxury however, it is a basic necessity that would take away many aches from our bodies, relationships and societies. How many emotionally balanced people initiate war? With all and everything being connected, it is especially important to bring your emotions into your awareness. If you think you have hardly any emotions, you may be sure you are repressing them and will get the bill in old age. Aging graciously is definitely possible, but it requires being aware of all that flows through you and all that you keep hold of, in your mind, in your heart, in your organs, tissues and bones. If you can move gracefully with life, life will move gracefully with you. So it is crucial to have respect for emotions, for the energy that moves through you. There is a whole different quality to life and happiness based on refusing or accepting emotions. If you observe them, learn to listen to them and give them the space to be, you will see that they are nothing to be afraid or ashamed of, on the contrary, you will see how genius they are. I primarily started to respect emotions on a mental level first thanks to the work of Riet Okken in 'The liberating power of emotions'. And indeed, the moments I feel I truly love them from within my heart, I experience a magnificent liberation and deep empowerment.

Emotions become most tangible when you feel them in your body. You might have pushed them away, having taught your mind to repress them and their message of a need for love. You might have built up a lot of emotional waste. But your body, however, never lies. Although it may vary a little for every person, Doctor Tim Brieske of the Chopra Centre describes this body language incredibly well: 'Fear may express itself in your body as a tight stomach or chest, cramps, coldness, shaking, weakness, or dizziness. Anxiety is chronic fear and shows as numbness, tuning out, irritability, and sleeplessness. The body may also feel listless or restless. Humiliation is similar to fear in that your body feels weak and sometimes shaky, but instead of feeling cold, you feel a wave of heat. You may blush and notice your skin growing warm. You might also notice yourself hunching over and drawing in, as though trying to disappear. Anger is most often manifested in the body as warmth and flushed skin, tense muscles, a clenched jaw or fists, irregular or quick breathing, an accelerated heartbeat, and a feeling of pounding in the ears. Hostility is like anger but requires no trigger to set it off. Instead, the body is constantly simmering, alert for the slightest excuse for full-blown rage. The body feels tight, tense, and ready for action. Frustration is like anger but is more pent up. It may feel like your body wants to lash out but does not know which way to turn. Your movements and posture may become rigid. Sometimes frustration is anger combined with denial. In this case, you will experience signs of denial, such as unusually rapid speech, shrugging, averted eyes, tightened jaw muscles, and shallow breathing. Guilt is a restless feeling. You may feel confined or suffocated with an overwhelming desire to escape. It might feel difficult to breathe, and your chest may feel tight or pressured. Shame is another heated feeling, accompanied by warm skin and flushed cheeks. However, there is also a sense of inner numbness that can paradoxically feel cold or empty. Like humiliation, shame can make you hunch and want to disappear. Depression feels cold and heavy. The body is lethargic and lacking in energy. Depressed people may feel cold much of the time. The body may move slowly, rigidly, or hesitantly, reflecting the condition of depression. And finally jealousy, a complex emotion that can contain elements of fear, humiliation, and anger. The experience of jealousy in the body will therefore vary a bit from individual to individual. You may feel the coldness, tight stomach, and pressure in your chest associated with fear, or you may feel the heated sensations that come with anger and humiliation.'

In the beginning learning about your emotions can be quite hard. But you start at the beginning. Just like reading once started with one letter and now you can enjoy beautiful stories. The main thing you have to pay attention to, is that emotions have a personal purpose, we just have not treated them as such. Taking responsibility for your emotions is not the easiest job, but it is not the most difficult one either. When you start, you will see few people are capable of truly taking responsibility for their emotions. It is how we have been trained. If you know that most people get stuck at the emotional level of a four-year old, because of lack of guidance and training, you will start to see that you actually keep playing out the painful experiences you had as a child. As a child you were rarely given the power to do something about your situation. Most of us were raised by a strict parental law. Whether it was a wise and supportive one or not, it was just the way it was, no questions allowed. Now you can ask questions and lift yourself out of that age and release the old experiences of power, play and love with the mind and power of an adult. Know that your partner or other people close to you are the ones you have chosen to jointly grow into truthful beliefs about life, about how to live life as a woman, a man and together. We learn from imitation, we imitate actions, not words, both the external and internal actions. This is the reason why it is so important to heal your inner child first before bringing more into this world.

## Shining mirrors and projections

In the beginning you may have the tendency to blame others for your pain as we are not used to taking responsibility for our inner world. When that happens, remember that the people around you help you to open your wounds and clean them properly, only to stitch them again so they can heal beautifully. In the same way, you will often see that others project their emotions and lack onto you until they take full responsibility for their pains. In the public arena this is what happens to people who stand in the spotlight. People pin all kinds of characteristics to celebrities and it has nothing to do with who they are. This happens in tiny villages and in Hollywood. Again this is a natural law, as shadows look for light, waiting and wishing to be seen. You might do the same, as projection is the most common compensation, also called a defense mechanism for not dealing with emotions. Projection for example makes you put your shortcomings outside of you and project them onto another person: 'They are not adaptive enough.' Introjection makes you swallow someone else's emotions and neglect your own: 'My parents often told me I was a bad child when I pushed their boundaries'. With retroflection the emotions you did not express towards someone else can come back to you like a boomerang: 'I never dare to express my anger when someone offends me, which makes me angry with myself'. With dissociation you retreat in a fantasy world: 'I have this group of friends and we are always in harmony and peace with each other'. In all, the quicker you respond to someone without taking any time to contemplate what is happening on a deeper level, the more certain you can be you are acting unconsciously, having a reaction, instead of an action. Only when you take time to breathe and stay or become still, which some people can do in a fraction of a second, can you change reactive behaviour into creative behaviour. The letters in these words may be similar, yet they convey a whole different world.

This projection mechanism can prove to be difficult, especially for highly sensitive people when they are not trained. Although we are all built to connect and learn individually and collectively by imitation via our mirror neurons, these people have more mirror neurons than average. Highly sensitive people pick up everything and since few people have learned to master their emotions in our culture, they are confronted with so many energetics, they might not know which feelings and emotions are theirs anymore. But whatever level of sensitivity you have or have developed, you have to master all kinds of energies. Only then you can differentiate your inner world from other people's inner world, you can learn who you are, and who they are, and you can set healthy boundaries. It is not up to you to carry the emotions of others on your shoulders, as this is false compassion and actually weakens not only you, but the other one as well. Unfortunately, it happens very regularly that people carry loads that are not theirs to carry. They tiptoe around the other, are submissive to the other's hot flashes, feel sorry for them and try to overly help them or please, always fulfilling the other's unhealthy needs. When you carry another person's pains, you deprive them of the possibility of growing into wholeness, of becoming deeply happy, as the only way to heal and deal with emotions and your true nature, is going through the emotions. So it may be your emotional lesson to be at ease with the pain of others and the roads they follow, and shift your focus from mere compassion for the person to compassion for yourself too, and balance them out. Learning how to deal with conflicts constructively will strengthen you profoundly and make your road much lighter and easier. This requires you to digest all your experiences where there was no such thing as a 'we' to support your being. The essence of conflict management is that you keep hold of the 'we' without losing the 'I'. This starts inside, uniting yourself with your higher self, which you can then effortlessly realize outside of yourself.

If you pay attention to it, you will see that at the beginning on the road to more consciousness many of your thoughts and actions are guided by other people's emotions, feelings, thoughts and opinions. This is a very natural tendency in our journey to find true love. If you are raised in a culture that has no self-responsibility for the inner and outer world, a person will project his unknown pains, the ones he does not want to, or cannot take responsibility for yet, onto another person. This places the load on someone else's shoulders. Here you recognize the patriarchal way of externalization, an unbalanced act on how to deal with emotions. If you find yourself in such circumstances it is very important to not get confused, stay in your center and let the emotions stay where they belong. This state of staying in your own energy field, of standing strong in the midst of a conflict, however, already requires quite some training. Confusion fades the more you have learned yourself about e-motions, energies in motion. As long as you have energetic weaknesses, others will mark them for you so you can work on them and put an end to the leaks. If you can see it like that, you can be grateful to the partner, child or colleague who pushes your buttons. You can thank them out load, laugh at your humanity and become each other's biggest supporter in fitting the leaks to become strong rivers that flow back into the sea.

Thus our emotions are triggered by outside events, triggers that wake us up and make us look inside. And so it takes a vigilant alertness to learn how to interpret all energies happening inside and outside of you. Moreover, when emotions are still running away with you, instead of you having emotions, they will completely colour your reality. Meaning that you cannot see things for what they really are. Words are not heard or switched entirely. A story is built upon the foundations of the ones written before, mostly already in childhood, and they no longer have anything to do with the present, but are a mere repetition of an old wound. When someone is not ready to take responsibility for their emotions or wounds, they have a hard time with the truth. Stories are created in the mind with the intention of not having to face the energies that are moving within. This is how scapegoats or enemies are created. Many fundamentalists operate in such a way. In reality, every religion and every person longs to meet God, longs to be part of the endless stream of love and feel one yet yourself. But it requires courage to see what is holding you from experiencing this loving stream and oneness, or what you are withholding from another. Truth is never hard, truth vibrates gently. It is the way with which truth is received or perceived, that is experienced as hard or gentle. Hence, the messenger often gets shot. It is important to realize that when someone is not ready for the message of truth, you should not get caught in their inner fight. For they will try to externalize their internal conflict, their acting upon an untruth, anything not to have to deal with that pain. In the beginning it is easy to be seduced into such a game, for it is the way you have been taught to deal with pain too, first focus on the others, then on yourself. But with a firm resolve of personal responsibility, and if needed some post-its on your walls, you will get the hang of it and step through, step out, or stay out of emotions easily, so you can follow your path others are here to assist you on and grow deeper into the truth and love you set out for at the start of your journey. It helps to always try to remember your commitment and desire for a deeply fulfilling life.

A very valuable insight for myself to enable this is that the quality of the way you receive a message is not dependent on the quality of the message itself. When you decide to be open to what you are yet to learn to be whole, you are empowered. You learn to see through the form and into the core. When you commit to seeing the sacred, the important insights that are hidden in messages, you transform yourself from an unconscious receiver into a conscious receiver. When confronted with the emotional chaos of another person, you can then connect to them with compassion and decide from a balanced point of view how to further relate to this, and eventually grow to a state of deep love.

## Power and powerlessness

Sometimes it is challenging to stay in power and graciously navigate the oceans of emotions. Women have been labeled as irrational or hysterical, being blamed for our human emotionality. It is a consequence of not being taught emotional intelligence or respect for a woman's ever changing and transforming true nature. When people externalize their fear for emotions, they do this in an attempt to shed their failure or lack of competence in dealing with it. Such events showcase insensitive masculinity and its counterpart irrational femininity, intolerant rationality versus sensational emotionality. When you know that they feed each other and form a circle, you can refrain from getting caught into it. Quite often both men and women show their desires counter intuitively, like pushing each other away when you want nothing more than to be closer together.

Looking into the word hysterical clarifies a lot. In Latin 'hystericus' means 'of the womb', in Greek 'hysterikos' means 'of the womb, suffering in the womb'. The movie Hysteria portrays lightly how hysteria, strong unmastered emotionality, once was seen as a woman's disease. Now we know it is nothing but the effect of unhealthy intimacy. As a woman, you might feel powerless when your partner is not open to understanding your emotions or needs. Whereas your partner may feel powerless for not being capable of doing anything about your seemingly sudden changes of emotions, being incapable of understanding it or guiding you back to a state of ease and peace. Sometimes men and women actually even make emotions a power game, emotionally blackmailing each other, playing a game of dominance and submission, mostly unconsciously. Healthy intimacy on the contrary means having a healthy emotional bond, being able to truly connect. In an intimate sexual relationship, it is in the womb our energies meet each other and so it is women and men together who are responsible for peace in the womb. Peace is realised when each heart and sexuality is developed, when both know how to connect and become one. Emotional intimacy does require courage and strength indeed. We are all products of our era, and both men and women have to look into their patriarchal conditioning and corresponding developmental level when it comes to being educated in living and dealing with emotions, love and sexuality honourably. In a patriarchal culture both femininity and masculinity get hurt. But when you learn how to use e-motions, you can transform the energy of powerlessness into the pure aligned power of your soul.

Another way for women to recognize their vibration of powerlessness is the experience of having been overpowered by masculine physical strength, leaving strong emotional imprints. Any woman can recall a moment that she felt afraid for her physical safety. For some this reason for fear, having sensed real danger, manifested into violence. Whatever version was yours, when you integrate it, knowing that powerlessness and power are two sides of the same coin, you master true core power. The more submissive you are as a woman, the more dominant the man you will attract and vice versa. It is a natural law that aids you in restoring your balance. Your relationship helps you to finish childhood and family history, it may be difficult to be grateful for your partner bringing you to your pain body and vice versa, but after the healing you can truly and freely relate to each other as the man and woman you are in origin. The only thing necessary to reach this in a relationship, is to ensure that the wish and action of looking deep into your hearts, comes from both sides. You are in a relationship together, your problems become his problems and vice versa, you do not need to solve them for each other, on the contrary, but support and respect for the relationship, from both sides is a prerequisite for a healthy loving relationship and self-image.

As long as we keep struggling to get this right, we will keep being confronted with the worst expression of relating until we truly grasp what we are to learn. Lots of good things are happening but there is still quite a road ahead. One in three women is raped or beaten at least once in her lifetime. We know about the hard number in South-Africa, where on average, every four minutes a woman is raped, and on average every eight hours a woman is murdered by her partner or a family relative. In Africa there are at least three thousand traditional cultural practices that go against women's rights. But in the West too, one in five women is still confronted with domestic physical violence. Officials are aware that the reported numbers do not correspond with the actual cases. Not honouring women for their feminine qualities leads to much emotional pain. Lakshmi Puri from UN Women put it beautifully, 'Culture, tradition and religion cannot and may not be called for to justify violence against women'. If we are to solve this issue, we should follow Einstein's saying 'You cannot solve an issue at the level of thinking that created it'. This requires for us to go from a patriarchal thinking level, to a holistic thinking level as an entire society. Although no violent actions should be condoned, it is important to understand that when a man acts out violence against a woman, physically, emotionally, mentally or spiritually, this does not necessarily mean he has no loving heart. It is much more complex than that. Only a bleeding heart can act out violence. When someone has experienced violence and did not have the support or teachings to completely digest it, the body locks it in. With the right triggers, mostly not in proportion to the force of the violence itself, it will show and come out again, ready to be dealt with. Only you yourself can choose to restore the innate capacity to feel safe and loved. And as such, be a true protector on all levels, physical, sexual, emotional, mental and spiritual, to even balancing them all. Men who have transformed to such a depth, are among the strongest of all. In the same way you have the capacity to be whole again after having suffered from violence. You can decide to become a woman of magnificent depth and power. On the road to true authenticity we are to integrate every vibration that is part of life.

Our culture carries the traits of violence and hostility, whether we like to admit it or not. We have a history of crusades and other wars in our genes, it is inherent to a patriarchal system that is out of balance. Violence is defined as 'Every action, or threat that goes with it, that violates the right of self-determination, self-development, physical and sexual integrity of people'. How can the so called democratic West claim to be non-violent and pro peace when feminine energy in itself is still being repressed in such a hidden and subtle way, that we women do not even notice it anymore? We have become so accustomed to violence, especially violence of the invisible realm, that we can no longer perceive it. It is pretty confronting as a Western woman to find out that violence has always been a part of your life, that war and domination are still glorified. There is no glory in only worshipping the rational mind.

There is no glory in portraying women selling themselves naked as objects. But there is a way out, a way to balance and integrate these energies. Being violated is the passive, feminine part of not loving yourself. Acting out in violence is the active, masculine part of not loving yourself. They always find each other. These two sides are both actively violating themselves on the inside. To reverse this they need to say no simultaneously to the violence within, choosing for the noble feminine and masculine part. Being violated, or acting out in violence, makes you feel ugly or unworthy. Paradoxically enough it actually helps you to learn how to be beautiful and worthy from your core. Like the 14th Dalai Lama once said, 'Violence is a complicated thing.' Research has shown that in violent situations, men mostly project their weaknesses onto women. In return, women often act too forgiving. Being forgiving and too passive is not true compassion. Do not lose yourself in being only feminine. Let go of idiotic compassion and choose real empathy, as real empathy protects and never harms, including yourself. To assert yourself you need your masculine power too. It is vital that you take care of yourself, first and foremost. If necessary, look for help while learning, within or without, since sometimes our challenges are bigger than ourselves. It is a sign of power that you see that. How should you look at your natural healthy aggressive energy, the same one that keeps a house warm, comfortable and nourishing? When I tell you that it is the same power that germinates a seed, that it is proportionate of your power to defend your children and their environment intelligently, can you be proud of your fire then? Will you finally start using your fierce power then? Will you start using it for yourself, and as such exude it to all those who surround you? Will you nourish them with what they deeply long for? Do you dare be a strong woman? When you experience violence in your life, it is an invitation to learn to direct your fire and strengthen your stance, to protect your space, your true identity, your integrity and your values, stand up for yourself. Will you learn to master your inner mother and father energy, to install safety and security? The mother energy that sweetly and unconditionally loves you and takes care of you when you get hurt or make a horrible mistake, and the father energy that creates an environment that keeps you safe from harm. The 'mother' is the protector of the inner well-being, the 'father' of the outer well-being. If we were not taught these natural and balanced vibrations by our caretakers, we have to teach them to ourselves and dream ourselves into being.

## Forgiving history

On the path of raising yourself in emotional literacy, your forgiveness is your freedom, over and over again. When you forgive the people who hurt you, you take away their power. Understanding and freeing yourself from your past, liberates your mind and body. It stops the cycle of making the same mistake in the present that once created the problem. Healthy relationships require communicating authentically, from your heart. You are to learn to listen to your partners feelings on a deeper level. It is giving I-messages instead of you-messages. It is realizing that every reproach is a desire wanting to be fulfilled. For some years I lived at a beautiful spot in Antwerp, at the old harbour. The city's red light district was only a five minute walk away. For a long time I did not like the way men felt when I passed by, especially not on a Saturday evening. At that moment of the week the vibration was the ugliest. When it was dark outside and I passed by, I carried an aggressive hostile protective energy, the kind that says 'leave me alone or I will kill you'. But I got tired of feeling that and one day

I realized these men's true need, their need for connection to the feminine. I decided to experiment with it and changed my own vibration when walking by. Instead of looking down on them I started looking at them gently, like men, boys really, wanting their mothers love but looking for it in the wrong place. And instantly the eyes and the energies of the men who looked at me, turned gentle and honourable. To others I even became invisible. I had found a new form of protection. Inside I thanked these men for admiring my femininity. For loving and looking for the beauty of a woman, even when they first showed it to me in a way I experienced as insulting and demeaning. When a man has no examples of how to honour a woman and the feminine, when he does not know how to contact his inner feminine side, you can be sure he will approach a woman in all the wrong ways, not understanding what he is doing wrong. And similarly so will a woman approach and attract men in all the wrong ways. When you allow both desires, a woman's desire to be honoured in the beauty of all her femininity and a man's desire for being allowed to honour the beauty in a woman, you stop fighting. When you allow a man to express himself, even when it is done in an infantile but respectful way, you honour and support a man in his masculinity. When you allow an emotion on its own, you can learn to detach the emotion from the images or stories that sustain it and you can receive the message. When you learn to let go of your personal desire and accept what life gives you, then it transforms you and naturally grants you your desires. Just let it flow through you and let it go, even the difficult parts. Let go what is old and dying and replenish it with something new that is stronger and more vital, like following the natural movement of life-death-rebirth.

The more refined you are as a woman, the more refined

your man's masculinity will become. This also works in the other direction and you can play and grow together as long as you like. A man's brain is wired differently than a woman's. Whether this is an original physical difference or one that came into being as a consequence of culture or not, as neurologist Cordelia Fine investigates insightfully, I leave to the researchers. In stress a man goes into fight or flight mode, with a woman, her limbic system gets activated, the part responsible for one's emotions. This means that a woman naturally activates more emotional links to get rid of stress. A man runs off and focuses on something else or beats it down energetically or physically. When the indication of stress is not used constructively both men and women return to a lower level of development. A level presumably without the danger of being confronted with their blind and growth spots. With emotional stress you can imagine you get extra fireworks on both sides. More specifically, it is the amygdala in the brain that becomes active when there is a negative response to something emotionally arousing. 'It is connected physiologically to different parts of the brain in each sex', states neuroscientist Sandra Witelson. In men it communicates intensely to motor parts of the brain, meaning behavior that is directed outward to the external environment, the fight or flight response. In women the amygdala is connected intensely to the hypothalamus, which is fed by the thalamus that transmits sensory perceptive information. The hypothalamus takes care of our internal environment, our breathing, our heart rate, our internal balancing system, and our emotions. It helps control our involuntary body functions, like our body temperature, appetite and sleep. A woman is thus wired to handle more internal links which makes it more complex to get back to homeostasis. Our emotional complexity is a source of exquisite guidance and beautiful mystery too. When your emotions tell you to pay attention to a certain aspect of life and you realize the root of the problem, take back the solution with you, and turn into the most stable aspect of your core again, you master change. In the end there is only one way to deal with emotions and that is going through them, whatever discomfort they may bring. If you can feel emotions without projecting them outwards, they truly empower you. Luckily, we also have our men. Since a man's focus goes more outward, he has a bigger capacity for not being overwhelmed emotionally. On average a man is more stable emotionally. Is it not wonderful when your man can ease your emotional reaction with one simple stable masculine look, word or hug? For balancing his emotional world and connecting to yours, however, he needs to practice more to set these inner links and make more active connections in his brain. These connections come more naturally to women. We truly complement each other beautifully. Nevertheless, these days, with all the attention focused outside, both men and women need a lot of inner time to restore their system. And to develop love, the most natural antidote to stress.

## Bonding joyfully

Many of us grew up in family systems that were not emotionally balanced. In circumstances where adults still have strong emotional attachments to their mother and father, you may find a lot of projection of these attachments onto the partner. You may find yourselves projecting all the unresolved issues with your parents onto each other as you have no other means to unconsciously tell your stories that way. Besides being alert for stories that do not match current reality, you can also see the patterns in other women and men who have passed by in your live. When people play out traumas, going into their reptilian brain, you can see them watching a movie inside their head, reliving old undigested emotions from the inside, making them further believe it is really happening again, or a version thereof. Even with different actors or set-ups, the same energy circulates, sometimes even lies are created to uphold their story. When this happens and no self-consciousness is present, there may be no impetus to listen mindfully, communicate maturely, or understand one another truly, or even see a loving hand or word for what it is. Clinically labeled, decompensation has kicked in, and there is no possibility for contact anymore. This happens to various degrees, depending on the level of consciousness, as few women and men have learned to bond healthily with their children. And of course, when we, women and men, were not raised healthily and do not take care of our movies, the circle will keep continuing.

With healthy bonding there are two main events in life. At the beginning of life a healthy mother bonds with her child from the very first moment. She feels herself and the child as one, preferably already at conception. It is important that a mother acts like a mirror for the child, not the child as a mirror for the mother on which she projects her expectations, fears and plans. Surely a child will mirror the unconscious behaviour of the mother and father too, but it is their job, being adults, to see which behaviour of the child actually comes from them and which from the child itself. A mother will only be able to feel and mirror her child's feelings, if she consciously feels her own feelings. If she neglects her own feelings, this will surely install contempt in her child for his or her own being. Not being mirrored as himself or herself deprives a child of respect, integrity, understanding and the feeling of being allowed to be instead of being in service of, and hence of any possibility to develop stable self-consciousness. Not being mirrored leads to a search in life until the mirror is found and the conditioned feelings of the mother can be released and make place for the own feelings, identity from without versus identity from within. Puberty is normally the moment in the child's development when a mother releases her child, both physically and emotionally. And so does the father. It is an essential for both parties to grow to the next phase. If you do not cut the umbilical cord energetically as a mother, a young person cannot develop his own unique energy field. If you naturally and gently release that bond, a teenager does not need to rebel or revolt, or subdue himself, he learns to walk independently in life and still feel safe that there are people who support him in his walk for freedom. It is then no longer an attached bond, but an independent yet connected bond.

When, as an adult, you still have to cut yourself loose, as your parents were never taught how to emotionally bond healthily with their children, you will reach out to another to take over the role your mother or father did not or could not take up. Although the choice to be each other's primal woman and man, is in its core a deeply loving outreach, this bond often goes with uncovering much suppressed pain. It may not be an easy, comfortable ride for either party. Growing into your woman or manhood will likely be with growing pains. Yet if you have already acquired the advanced skill of comforting each other in distressing moments, much energy can be saved. And if you remember that the pain is like a dirty spot on a window, and the clean window is your inner state of peace, you can clean it when the time is right. In essence it is actually a beautiful lesson in motherhood, one of the phases of womanhood, way before you are one. And for him in fatherhood. It is essential for a girl to have a father present, a man who knows how to manifest the protective energy of a man, showing and teaching how to set healthy boundaries. And so, as a woman, this masculine trait is essential to feel strong. So stand up for your boundaries and self-respect, give yourself the freedom to live and learn to work with e-motions. Be guided to the root of your emotions and uncover what is lying there waiting for you to bring into your consciousness. For sure it is always easier to see the other one's roots, but make yours your primal interest. Your communication will be incredibly essential, even when you speak the same maternal language. Check whether the words you use, convey the same world to you. When in a discussion, check that you are talking about the same thing. Check whether your tone of voice and body language correspond to your actual words and intention. Recognize your past, present and future. And when you have a negative message to communicate, check that you communicate it from your heart, from a place where you are more alike than different, as from there it will be easier heard and accepted without anger, contrary to sharing a negative message when you yourself are off center. Help each other uncovering what the mirror is saying to you. Your mirror is a great guide to freedom and liberty.

At the depth of these emotional prisons men and women are in, you may find a lack of grounded spiritual bonding too, a strong yearning for safety and security, for vitality and joy. When you believe you have no direct connection to the primordial energy that keeps you safe and strong, fear will permeate every layer of your life. Fear of emotions, together with all other things invisible, will keep you from your strong and stable core. This fear is the primal emotion to be released to open the road to your core. Emotional waves are a feminine energy, and feminine energy has been forbidden and desecrated for far too long, by both men and women. At the bottom of your emotions as a woman, you may come across shame for being a woman, for being a sexual creature, high numbers of breast cancer being an intuitively logical result of that, apart from the many external factors such as toxic foods and environments. You may find disgust, anger and sadness for the patriarchal system, even hopelessness as it has been existing for so long. When you open up to these emotions however, and live them fully, you will be able to connect again to the Divine Feminine, and to the Divine Masculine, femininity and masculinity in their purest form. It is essential to deal with the anger properly, for if not it will find another way out. The unhealthy masculine way will externalize it, the feminine internalize it, better known as resentment. Hence, living in a patriarchal system makes the undealt with emotion of anger double trouble for women. Women are given the anger of men, internalize it, and often dislike theirs on top of that. Being so cut off from their divine feminine, many women are weakened and have a lot of bitterness and other emotional pains to release and heal. This often stems from love affairs that changed them in a negative way, when they were cheated on or abused by a loved one. These are events in life which are just ways life helps you grow into your fullness, even when you feel broken to your primal core. It is up to you whether you take the invitation for fullness on or not. Blaming yourself or someone else, will not bring you to sweetness again.

So see this patriarchal era for what it has been, a growth phase to reaching wholeness. Learn to forgive life and learn to master its energies and forces. Released double trouble also means gained double power, remember that. Tears are a gentle way to cleanse yourself of emotions. Just like the rain waters the flowers and the trees, including the occasional thunder storms. The more you allow yourself to be open, the easier it all will flow. So always try to remember your wish for wholeness, as that is where your emotions want to take you. You and the other person. Take responsibility for the hurting part in you, for the possible lack of having grown up with a truly loving example, and know that with every healing you are one step closer to true love. The more whole you are, the more whole your relationships will be, the more whole society will be. Emotions are a deeply grateful guide to your authentic self. It is not an endless cycle, but a returning to your beginning and your core, consciously this time.

# Collective unconsciousness

Knowing that our material culture has not invested in feeling consciousness, you can expect quite some unpleasant surprises that are in dire need of love and care when you set out for rebalancing. Just like we inherit our physical genes, we also inherit our emotional, cultural and spiritual genes. The inner and outer consequences of having neglected feelings for so long are no surprises of course when you dare to open up to the dynamics of abandonment. They are merely the logical results of earlier actions. We are the sum of all that has been before us and at the same time the indicator for what our future holds. A society is the sum of its individuals and if we keep doing more of the same, as an individual and a collective, we cannot expect another outcome. If we want to prevent history from repeating itself, we are to face its hidden unwanted and rejected parts and transform them into love, on an individual and a collective level. It is the only way we can change history and dream it into a new one. To grow our consciousness, we can start learning in energetic awareness from the east. When we bring Eastern feeling awareness together with Western material awareness, then, as always where two opposites unite, a higher third version can be created. That is the natural law of polarity.

## Uncherished natural principles

It is but normal that, in our relationships, we play out the pains and frustrations of the typical role models of a patriarchal society. In its worst form it is played by irrational women who attach men to them via babies and by insensitive men who use women and nature as mere objects, the polar opposites of the pain of an uncherished femininity and masculinity. To release the judging character of blame and fault, so inherent to later Christian culture, we need to face this cultural trait openly to be able to truly let it go. It is about accepting the shadow of our masculinity and femininity, and uniting them within ourselves. As such it is not about whose fault uncomfortable leftovers are, but about stepping away from automatic reactions that keep us repeating that same old history. 'It is about realizing what you want now, about what you learn from the actual facts that happened, where you can take responsibility now, see your choices and possibilities in every moment and create win-win relationships', like Marilee Adams explains in 'Change your questions, change your life'. By recognizing the unconscious playing field, you can culturally re-educate yourself, you can create openness and step out of the circle of blaming, hurting and being hurt.

Men and women have not been taught the natural principles of feminine and masculine energies for a couple of thousand years. We keep fighting each other to find them again. Instead of being each other's enemies we need one another to realize the unity we each yearn for, within and without. We cannot do it alone. We need each other. It is not he or she, them or us, it is him and her, them and us. If there would be one style, it could only be a mixed style that connects to both ends of the spectrum. To live this unity we have to forgive all that has held us away from it. It means forgiving yourself for the pain you have caused others and forgiving others for the pain they have caused you. And on top of that, when you take full responsibility, it also means forgiving yourself for the pain you have caused yourself. Both men and women have to free themselves from the patriarchal image of a woman and a man.

How we relate to a person, whether in the private or the public domain, depends highly on how we perceive that other person, not on who he or she really is, unless you have an open consciousness of course. If we believe that someone does not really like us or is trying to hurt us, we will react very differently to that person compared to perceiving him or her as finding us a sympathetic person or reaching out. The Centre for Partnership Studies of Doctor Riane Eisler showed how our collective unconsciousness is marked by a dominant relationship model, where one partner is more valued than the other, and so the first relating pattern is much more common. But deep down, in each and every one of us, you can find a relationship model, where both are equally valued and know they cannot exist without the other. We can choose to evolve away from the dynamics of dominance, from a disproportionate control over someone, by just one of the poles initiating the action for change. The moment the powerless one comes into his or her personal power, the ruler is finished. The moment the dominator sits down and goes within to see from where this domination or manipulation comes, the dynamic shifts. Intimacy can then return in the relationship and this is exactly what everybody longs for so deeply. You can expect that when you set out for true love your bodily sensations will bring out all characteristics of the old dominant model that most of us still carry in our genes, characteristics that hamper the flow of deep love. Read it then, integrate it and let it go. Then you will be ready for what is called an equipotential relationship, 'Where every participant is seen as equal in the sense of them being both superior and inferior to themselves in varying skills and areas of endeavor, intellectually, emotionally, artistically, mechanically, interpersonally, and so forth, but with none of these skills being absolutely higher or better than others. It is important to experience human equality from this perspective to avoid trivializing our encounter with others as being merely equal', as expressed clearly by Jorge Ferrer, the chair of the department of East-West Psychology at the California Institute of Integral Studies and advisor to the organization Religions for Peace at the UN.

## Hidden feminine beauty

With the exception of some individual and country exceptions, how come that vibration of beautiful femininity is hardly to be found in our public arena anymore? How come that deep love, mutual support, care and unifying forces are no longer standard characteristics of our societal values, but have become conditioned to hard numbers and profit lines, even when so many people uphold these beautiful values? Inner feminine beauty, in all its facets has long been hidden and forbidden from the public scene, or shaped in such a way that it would fit a masculine mold, losing all its inherent beautiful qualities. Practically everything invisible, symbolic, integrative, holistic, experiential and uncontrollable was taken out of the equation. This giving the unconscious message that feminine beauty is ugly and should not come into the light, let alone come in to jointly lead a country. The beautiful made ugly, with enough push and domination you can change everybody's perception, on the surface.

Many had this message engrained in their cells and keep living up to it that way. The more these aspects were hidden, the more unfamiliar they became. Soon they were labeled bad too, an easier way to deal with something outstandingly powerful than to admit deep fear to such astounding power and beauty. How beautiful is the smell of a rose, the shimmering light of a rainbow, the attraction to a lover, the calling to journey to a faraway country, the intuitive insight that your friend needs help, calling her to find her in tears and somehow telling her wise comforting words that seem to come from another world? How beautiful is it to find new business ways to connect a whole planet in an integrative way, to use resources in a closed circle system, to use what once was trash to ignite an exquisitely designed car and have access to enough water, food and education for everyone at the same time? How beautiful is it to sit in a handmade wooden chair that makes you feel like a king or wear a dress that lifts you into queenship? How beautiful is it when the elders who still can touch upon the ancient folklore, are consulted about where the fairy folk live in order to divert highways around their communities? How beautiful is it when children are taught to develop their masculine intelligence in the morning and their feminine intelligence in the afternoon to unite it one day within? How beautiful is it that in difficult moments you can hear your deceased father comforting you with the wisest words? How beautiful is it to sense that you are protected and guided by wise creatures simply by asking for their help? How beautiful is it when you hear the trees speak? How beautiful is it when a child connects to so-called wild animals, and rests safely guarded in their presence? How beautiful is it to let the animals tell you how the weather is going to change or something dangerous is about to happen, and warn you if you only choose to listen to them? How beautiful is it to sense your own body is moving energies through you and healing you? How beautiful is it to learn to read symbols on ancient old pottery that tell about the energetic waves that flow through a woman's body? How wonderful is it when making love, you sense a goddess energy taking over you, melting in the arms of your man who has become the manifestation of the most powerful god? How wonderful is it to let nature take its course and believe, feel in every cell all will be well, that life will take you exactly where you need to be, and that you know you will possess all the necessary tools to deal with what life brings your way?

All this may seem chaotic and uncontrollable at first sight, but it holds the most stability and security I have ever touched upon, you just need to look a bit deeper. As a woman you can develop a direct connection to the primordial woman again, an energy field that fulfills your every need, that makes the entire world glow with a mysterious beauty that you can easily grasp. You can see connections and unfoldings that not everyone can yet, you can sense hidden emotions that taint business people's decisions or strategies, you can peak into possible futures, you are guided by higher forces and every day you are better at balancing and deeply enjoying life's forces. You do not need to go underground as an occult organization this time. This beauty is here for every woman to pick up again. In this era we are again part of the sages who carry the wisdom of the feminine. We support and co-lead our leaders, family, company and country, to make sure balance will become everybody's experience again.

# Balancing relaxation and tension

Obviously the absence of standard living feminine beauty finds its repercussions in our daily lives. I have been studying and working on sustainable development since university and became aware of a lot of solutions to current problems our world faces. Simultaneously I was confronted with all the tensions our global world carries. Sustainable development is about balancing the social and the environmental with prosperity for all. I worked at management schools and researched how to teach people this mindset. I learned a lot about managerial and technological innovations and applications, but at one point I wondered why the big shift had not happened yet? And then I came to understand that as long as man has no balance within, neither would we reach balance in the greater world.

## A tensed culture

When you see how many Western people are taking antidepressants these days, you need to ask questions, new ones, right ones. To me the most logical step forward was to trace its roots instead of finding it normal that more pills are prescribed to artificially adjust people's neurological systems again. There is no empowerment whatsoever in pills as the only approach. People have to learn to feel again, learn the wisdom their bodies hold and understand that we live in a culture where the stress-button is continually on, something you do not even notice anymore. Constriction has become the norm. It is created from anxiety, from an unhealthy ego state, whereas being expansive and open-minded is created from peace, from a soulful state. It is important to realize that the tension to earn ever more money is not going to make you happier or more open in the long run. In one of my relationships I was blessed with experiencing extreme richness for a while. It showed me very quickly that I actually did not want things anymore, that many of these material wishes were actually a desire created and puffed by our system and not a true longing from my heart. I had already learned how economics, advertising and communication work from the point of view of a company that is only about profits, but it was enriching to experience consumption from the point of view of being able to afford everything. I felt ever more clearly how our consumption society anticipates on your lack of wholeness. And every time this lack is addressed, a tension sets in your body. You supposedly need to work more and have more money to fulfill the artificially created void. It actually feeds on your lack of true love.

Financial independence is a wonderful state that gives you grounding, but it is not true that it can only be reached if you possess more than a million on your bank account. People who believe this and follow the path that richness will buy them happiness and fill the void, might get very disappointed. You can actually develop a deficiency in the necessary soul power to deal with worldly power harmoniously. As Daniel Kahneman says, 'Money does not buy you happiness, but lack of money certainly buys you misery'. Artificially fulfilled needs will never be satisfying, as a substitute never vibrates like the true need. Therefore such a way is hardly the ground to create stability on, not for yourself, nor for the planet. It does not leave much space for deep relaxation either. Conversely, when you connect money to your dharma, your contribution that is unique to your core, you can fill your life with positive energy. For in the end, that is what money is, a form of energy. To relax into it, you have to let go of any belief that making money is a painful thing. But that of course is not so easy in our current labour system.

If you know that a human being needs three consecutive weeks to truly rest and recharge his or her batteries, you can understand that we are working in a system that is not set to relieve you from your tension. To truly relax and feel your body sink into it, you need time. And time is not available in a masculine system guided by a mechanical clock. This exaggerated focus on masculine principles, on expansion and tension, linear thinking and straight lines is all around. It even forms the basis of what most of our cities are built upon. When you take a walk in Western cities, your eyes and mind are constantly influenced by these masculine principles. Neurologically you need more energy to process a straight line than an organic natural line that is omni-present in nature. This visual stimulation of straight lines constantly plays on only one part of your brain. The occasional tree and organic lines in the streets are not present enough to create a visual balance that stimulates your neurons, consciously or unconsciously. Hence, it is very normal and natural for your body and mind to tense up. And so the pills alone will not help.

## An enriching culture

To truly relax your body and get to sense your true nature again, you need to digest and release many conditionings. Sometimes they can be quite hidden. At my family home, although taught the principles of democracy, symbolized by the round table, in essence only our left brain thinking was invited and allowed to sit around the table, feelings and intuition were not. It was a rather rational democratic system, not yet an emotional democratic one. Only when I researched deeper, did I come to understand that there was deeper ground waiting to be touched. In so many places feelings and intuition are not listened to and silenced. Indirectly, but very clearly, the message is sent that they are not welcome. Hence, we are often taught to love differences only at a mental level, mental tolerance rather than true acceptance from the heart. It is a good start though, as there are still places where mental tolerance is not even an option. In the Western world there seems to be a politically correct way of dealing with differences. We are taught to make them work together rationally, but on a feeling level they are in fact often mocked, making us lose so much valid information on overlooking and connecting the entire system. Deep down all the intangible is often experienced as a source of tension, as an uncontrollable thing and hence feared. It is rarely experienced as a source of enrichment, or approached with a profound interest to learn about what the other deeply moves and what connects us all. In the formal Western schooling system there has been little or no room for differentiation outside the industrial productivity box. And it has long been considered among the best education systems in the world. But teaching is not only about successively accumulating knowledge. True teaching is about awakening consciousness. Hence, when you put the principles of indigenous education next to those of Western education, you get an extraordinary full spectrum that can handle a much wider range than we are capable of now.

Unfortunately, as all children can only follow one curriculum, have to behave in a certain way and sit still for eight hours a day, this will definitely create tension. You can easily see it in all the new dis-eases children supposedly have. But if you look closely, these are not the children's ailments, these are ailments of an educational system that does not fit its time anymore and has come to clearly show its flaws. A child naturally uses eighty percent of its right brain and only twenty percent of its left brain before going to preschool. These proportions switch entirely after only a couple of months at a traditional Western school. With new societal traits of high information load and access, the emotional aspects that go with this, less physical play and more technology, newly formed families, the digital age and its effect on the quality of relationships, a need to loosen old ineffective conditionings and rebalance the system is generated.

In the body too much tension, too much stress, too much yang, too much fire causes inflammation. You need cooling energy to balance that. You need water, yin, feminine energy. You need to enrich and refresh the environment. Neurologists Rubenstein and Merzenich found out that too much excitation, or not enough inhibition in the brain cells, create more irritability, hypersensitivity and overload leading to loss of informational complexity and organization. We experience more noise, more intensity and less signal. It is essential to reduce the amount of yang, so that the brain can get more bandwidth again. The glial cells that support and nurture our nerve cells, need to do just that instead of fighting off inflammation. Information will be better received and you can discern differences more easily. Research on Einstein's brain, the man who could bridge visible and invisible worlds, bridge left and right brain hemispheres, showed a heightened amount of glial cells. You can understand how important rest is in enabling them to function as they were intended in the first place. They are not intended to fight too much masculine energy to rebalance the system, on the contrary. Our children need space and time to just breathe, to just be.

So true change, therefore, is not a mere mental act, it requires change in the body, mind and spirit. If you allow yourself to be here in your very own authenticity, you will feel the happiest, most successful and most meaningful that you can be. Be different, be yourself. But to reach that authenticity, that state of flow, you are to let go of all built-up tensions on all levels. There are many ways to do this, the only essential part is that it is grounded in your body too. You will see that being aware and working with your body, is part of mindfulness. If not, you will soon find yourself in the same situation as before you started a mindfulness class, or started beating that cancer. Everybody can find his or her own way of releasing tensions physically. You can add even more yang, such as sports, which will make you go in excess and make you sleepy afterwards, or you can go about it more directly via feminine ways such as meditations, creative outlets or bodywork.

## Opening and releasing

When you start working with your body, you first have to make sure to not keep adding more tensions to your body. When you have worked enough and feel your neck tensing up, take a break. When you are confronted with your likes or dislikes, learn to neutralize them, accept them both, as loving goes beyond them. When you feel emotional, express them consciously so they can flow and you prevent them from getting stuck. When expressed unconsciously these chemically traceable cells will get stored in your body. And above all, consciously flow with your breath. Second, you will have to take old tensions out of your body. You could have felt very agile at one point in your life, and you can be tensed at another, even when you develop personally. The thing is that once you relax at one level, you are ready to go deeper into another and new deeper tensions can come to the surface. At every level you make your structure ever softer so that you can get in. And the levels and experiences of conditionings will keep coming until you touch upon your true core, where you are relaxed in yourself and at peace with your surroundings. It is altogether, your awareness that transforms tension into relaxation, which can be done at a very high speed when mastered.

In itself tension is not a bad thing, it is harmful only when it is out of balance with relaxation. We have both relaxed and tensed muscles when we lift something with our arms, they work together to create something. So tensions bring you to an ever deeper state of creation of and being in life. In cranio sacral therapies for example the release of tensions shows in many ways, your body knows how to do it. This type of therapy just activates and offers the support for your self-healing system to do what it is here for you. You can get hot, or very cold, you can get an itch, a bubble, a jerking of a muscle, tears or a memory popping up. Our body intelligence is so miraculous, it knows perfectly which muscles to tense for another to relax deeper and it has a thousand ways to restore its balance.

In the beginning you might need support to teach your body how to relax to let go of tensions, somebody will need to help you hold a space for you. All people that work on the energetic level know how to create a loving field for you to feel safe, relax and let go. And after a while when you know how to relax deeply and set your self-healing in motion you can be your own doctor. It is no longer necessary to become ill for you to become aware of a problem. For disease is actually the final warning system of us humans. It is an energetic problem deeply engrained, deeply tucked away in the physical that shows itself throughout life until ready to be released. So your illnesses indicate where in your body you hold energetic blocks, they give you an indication how you connect the physical with the energetic and if you are alert you can notice the links to your way of relating to yourself, to dear ones, to your thoughts, your emotions, your choices, in all to your behavioural patterns and through the lens with which you see life.

When you are relaxed and open you can receive intuition and dreams on which direction to take in life, direction that is in line with your core, or that guides you to your core. But when your mind is cluttered, such subtle information goes unnoticed. So the information will look for another road to reach you and will present itself a little more explicitly, first via positive emotions and then via negative ones. And if you really are a hard learner or listener, or when the road is so tough, your body will make sure you will not be able to move anymore and oblige you to go within and deal with it. That is the reason of existence of disease. Paradoxically, it is not something that fights you but is working for you, for the aliveness of your core. We humans really are of an exquisite nature.

The more you relax, the more you can open yourself, the more you can surrender to the flow of life, the easier, the more wonderful and the more purposeful and loving the ride is. This openness is an essential quality to come into a state of receptivity, to enter the feminine realm. This openness has an unconditional loving quality. In it, trust that you feel what you feel, whether painful or blissful. You can always tap into it when putting your consciousness in the now, in the present moment. Receptivity is a feminine quality and of very high importance, the masculine gives, the feminine receives. When you are relaxed and open, you can receive information that is extremely subtle and of an astounding beauty.

# The cycles of nature

To be deeply open and receptive thus requires relaxation, only then can we let the flow of life and its intelligence follow its own current. That is the way nature does it, and the way it works for us too. When we go against the cycles of nature, the system will adapt, yet it keeps its inherent original intelligence. It is the same with our bodies. We all know how important it is to have a healthy circadian rhythm for restorative sleep and a vital and happy waking time. Even when you have been on sleeping medication, with the proper care you can always reset your rhythm in its natural state. Similarly, when we as women use contraception that interferes with the natural hormonal cycle of a woman, we may lose contact with our most powerful source, our connection to our original intelligence, the embodiment of nature. A nature that knows, loves and lives the cycle of life-death-rebirth. Yet, we can always choose to connect to this inherent original intelligence once again.

## Manufactured cycles

In 2002 the Environmental Toxicology Program of the National Institute of Environmental Health Sciences in the US confirmed that the entire group of steroid estrogens is carcinogenic. Not only millions of women and female adolescents take the pill, but its substances also get into our drinking and ground water through them, affecting children, men and other women. In 1990 researchers Romieu and co did a meta-analysis of 21 studies researching the influence of oral contraception done since the 1980s, which stated that women who had taken the pill for 4 years or more before their first pregnancy, had a 72% higher risk of getting breast cancer.

Another study conducted by Olsson and co showed findings that when young women, who had taken the pill or had an abortion at a young age, develop breast cancers with tumors that are more dispersed, more aggressive and they therefore have a shorter life expectancy. When you add to that that one out of three women undergoes an abortion somewhere in her life, hormonal contraception can be a malignant form of protecting the sexual freedom of women and their health. The Institute Reinier De Graaf added all the information and found that, in the end, cervical and liver cancer are more likely and that the lowered risk of ovarian and endometrial cancer is rather relative. Nevertheless, many doctors and gynecologists continue to prescribe the pill as a healthy contraception. The pill was invented in the fifties, a time we had little knowledge about a woman's sexuality or of the energetic importance of her fertility process for her health and her personal and collective development.

These synthetic hormonal influencing techniques have also been used to presumably fight the effects of menopause. As a result of that, women of an older age had to deal with carcinogens in their system for a second time. Based on the collected studies in 2002 the Women's Health Initiative that worked on the effects of estrogen and progestogen substitution therapy with postmenopausal women was aborted abruptly. In an up market town in Belgium, in 2012, a radiologist stated that one out of five women there have breast cancer, proof that Western medicine currently knows very little about certain aspects of life and health, and highlights much needed room for growth.

Of course there are very often as many studies confirming the pros as there are confirming the cons, as that is a big part of science's set-up, yet let this information support you in understanding the difference you feel being on the pill or not. I feel that letting your natural hormones follow its course helps you ground your true feminine nature, they aid you in giving you the messages you need to struggle or flow through life. The more natural you are living, the more naturally their information will come to your consciousness, the easier your entire body will work to make it an enlivening ride. If you have diverted your body from its natural path, you can easily choose to get back into the saddle and direct it back to the main road again.

To help your body be strong or recover, it is important to support your detox organs, your liver to detox the estrogens, and your lungs and kidneys too. 'Your colon is highly important too, there is apparently no such thing as a cancer patient with a healthy colon', says cancer specialist Doctor Josef Issels. It is vital to keep our hormonal system healthy, it is so important for our health, and pleasure and peace too. Orgasms for example produce the happy hormones oxytocin, vasopressin and endorphins. And also dopamine plays a leading role in this situation, as it is involved with the foreplay, the motivation, the attention and the accessability of enjoyment.

Luckily there are also people in Western medicine that take these and other indicators into account and so a group of German researchers have developed the Sensi©-plan. It was not that easy to find a good alternative to the pill, but this is to me the best system yet. It taught me, at the age of 31, many things about my femininity. Whether women use this system or another, it should be taught in schools for girls to learn to know their body, how it works and how you can read its signals. Women are not as unpredictable as we are led to believe. On the contrary, once you are capable of, yet again, reading the subtle information, it is easy to recognise your personal cycle and your body's signals. Your temperature, your cervical fluids, your energy level, your skin, your mood, your breasts, your sexuality and even your dreams are all signals that tell you about your cycle. Moreover, fertility problems in adulthood would drop instantly as you learn about your creative process. As that is what it is. It may take up to nine months for your cycle to find its natural balance again after hormonal contraception, so imagine how it must be for you and your baby if you get pregnant within that period, it would mean a double hormonal shifting for your body and a stressful environment for the baby as well. But that can easily be prevented. On the one hand if you know all this, you will no longer take fertility for granted and on the other hand, as you have learnt to let your body intelligence work for you conceiving will come more naturally.

## Natural cycles

The beauty about this system is that the responsibility of fertility does not only lie with the woman, it requires the man's involvement too. It inherently teaches you responsibility for the power you hold together, and this enhances a relationship naturally. A man can truly get to know his woman, stating that unpredictability hence has more to do with not understanding how cycles work. The female body in its natural state cannot just go around and have sex all the time without physical consequences. Of course on a deeper level this goes for a male body too. Contacting and honouring your body in its natural state again is very empowering, it makes you aware of what creative power you hold. And this is not limited to the physical level.

On the physical level there are two periods, one before and one after the ovulation. Each period is characterized by another hormone, in the first one estrogens rule and in the second progesterone. Testosterone is also produced in our ovaries, and our adrenal glands, it helps us maintain muscle and bone strength. All these hormones influence our sexual drive and even our tendency to use our left or right brain, to focus outside or within. On an energetic level however, you can speak of four periods, each with its own characteristics, just like the major moon phases. In more detail we can see eight phases of the moon cycle. The new moon represents the beginning, the waning crescent immersion, the last quarter contemplation, the waning gibbous co-operation, the full moon culmination, waxing gibbous assessment, first quarter action, and waxing crescent growing to return to the beginning. If you listen to and honour this flow, your body and your inner world will flourish. It is not that women were handpicked by God Almighty when they were handed out bad flows and post menstrual symptoms, they have their roots and reasons too. Symptoms are not to be mistaken as causes. During your period you get sensitized more deeply, you can notice much easier what lies buried inside of you. In this phase your emotional body awakens more strongly. Unfortunately most of the women have a painful emotional body, not a happy emotional body and this can make your period very uncomfortable. By taking care of your energetic world however, you can influence the ease of your cycle, to a point that it sweetly flows.

Energetically your menstruation is characterized by an inner-inner energy, meaning that it is a time for reflection and attention to your inner world. Your senses are heightened and it is easier to receive subtle information since your body is fully open. Your intuition is at its highest, receiving information from all over your body and beyond. In traditional cultures women were given the time to use this power. The women were not expelled for being unclean, but they withdrew in the forests to have their reflective time, to reflect on their life and growth during the past moon. Your period is a moment to not only let go of unused physical material, but also to cleanse and release your system from any emotional, mental or spiritual loads, you and your body reborn.

In some cultures women retreated in turtle houses, a safe haven open to women only. The elder women would take care of the children granting their daughters and women time to strengthen themselves and so the entire tribe. Women had time for their children. They had time for themselves. The responsibility was carried by the right people, allowing children and women to feel the lightness of life. Reverence was not given to the young, but to the wise of heart and experience, the ones who knew how to respond to life. Maybe we do no longer have the means of community living like this, or not yet again, but it must be doable to standard give yourself one day of your menstruation purely for yourself, and when you have a deeply loving man who is knowledgeable about the natural laws, he will gladly assist you to realize this you-time every month, as he will easily notice the advantages for him and your children when you are being given your sacred time every month. And what about work you say? Well yes, this system that has lacked any form of feminine energy will slowly move along if you stand up for it to make it move along. Or become independent. You will see that when you truly retreat, without television, books or any other stimuli, you are given the opportunity to tap into your creativity, deeply, it is productivity in pure feminine form. And when nature shows you it is time to come out of your retreat, you take with you your feminine contribution to society.

The period after your menstruation then knows an inner-outer energy. You look for ways to contribute to the world, how to link what you have learned from your intuition within with the outside world, you look for the right people to materialize it with and what is required to manifest it. You can roughly say that each period is about a week.

In the third period you are full force focused on the outside world, it is an outer-outer energy, very masculine in nature. Your physical power is also at its highest here and if you use it to your advantage, this is a time you can easily have a lot of labor done without any effort. Of course when you are working on manifesting personal growth, it is about manifesting energies and insights in the world. In all it is about putting in practice what inspired you from within to be created in this world.

And with the fourth period you make the circle round, the direction of your energy is an outer-inner energy. You take all you have learned and the new information life gave you, and slowly you start going within to reflect on the further path to take. Here you have a good view on what you have given life to and you gradually start to evaluate your creation.

## The power of creation

This process of creation is a natural law, whether you are conscious about it or not. Unfortunately few women are, losing the experience of extraordinary beauty. Too many women, and men, still carry so much pain, they are so completely enveloped in their own pain they cannot even see how they harm others in their current. Being unfulfilled as a woman, meaning being unfulfilled in your own nature, in your own creative process to birth your authentic self into this world, can make you create fulfillment in a mere material external way, without your inherent feminine spirit. Women who are not yet masters of their creative powers, often create a baby to fill a void that they feel inside, quite often even without the consent of the chosen man. This type of fulfillment will not last very long of course. Similarly, it is not strange that women who have not yet been able to conceive themselves, are jealous about those who have for they are still to learn to master their own creative process. How outstanding is it when they have finally learned this mastery too, are pregnant and radiate a serenity and love that we all may enjoy. We all carry the consequences of our power of creation, and it is up to ourselves whether we create light ones or heavy ones, positive ones or negative ones. This power is always here for us, to teach us, to grow, to live. Its main reason for existence is to bring you to a life of deep joy and happiness, a wonderful gift put inside of you, whether you go via the shadow or via the light, as both doors serve their purpose to this end. And at every moment you can change direction if you choose to. If you use this power consciously and take into account the consequences for you and others, you can contribute in marvelous ways that benefit everyone who comes into contact with your creations.

Therefore, the more fulfilled you are, the more full your creations will be. And every system longs for loving flowing energy, every system thrives on high vibrations of wholeness. In some cultures women were said to carry the energies of the sun and the moon. In the West, this power of creation and fullness into femininity is shown in the symbolism of moon goddesses where each goddess represents a phase of the moon, and each phase is to be integrated to become a whole and full-on woman. Marijke Baken writes in 'The way of Inanna', that the virgin goddess shows the power to stand on your own, your fullness, you feeling one is not dependent on a relationship with a mate, you have made your masculine and feminine energies one. There is no need to please, to be approved, or adapt to the wishes of another, there is only the wish to act in accordance with the truth. And she knows how to refrain or reiterate from demeaning the virgin into a helpless girl.

The mother goddess carries the power to preserve and protect life, she holds the power to nurture, unite and support in sustainable ways. This motherhood is to be taken broader than the mere biological sense. The mother goddess shows how to care for your own power and passion, your joy and vitality. She knows what to let go of to support growth into maturity, and owns the wisdom of her body. She knows how to keep her from becoming a self-sacrificing caring creature.

The crown goddess shows the power of transformation and death, how to welcome separations, death, things that pass, and metamorphosis. She knows when to bring them forth, whether in a job, a learning period, a journey, a relationship, in society. Hence in her deepest aspect she is also called the death goddess. She represents the ways of knowledge that germinate out of the shadow, the darkness, winter, intuition, signals or self-knowledge. She holds the wisdom that the cycles of change are inherent to nature, she knows how to creatively move with the change, whether it happens in an orderly fashion or in a complex and chaotic way. The crown goddess holds the gifts of interconnectedness, freedom, openness and surprise of all possibilities. She knows how to refrain from choosing only the light side of life. In the east these goddesses are known as the birth-giving Maya, Durga the preserving Mother and Kali Ma the death-dealing crone.

# Our core

Our belly, the feminine uterus is the physical symbol for the connection to the goddess and her creative power. Women are the keepers of the creative process, in the physical way for growing babies, and much more than that, it is also available for babies that take the shape of a company, a project, or a feeling too. That is why in the old days women's intelligence and energy of gestating and growing were essential in shaping society, for they could easily tap into the creative power, as if they had a direct link to the divine built into their body. They could easily match the invisible world with the visible world. Every month they would be granted easy access, a perfect way for balancing the inner and the outer world. And when women reached menopause, with all their cosmic guidance put into practice in their life experiences they supported society in a more passive way, advising how to go about with certain dealings in life, leaving the active work to the younger generations.

For sure men can get access to these balancing cosmic vibrations as well, that is what meditation is for. We are after all, all made up of yin and yang energies. We women just have one very special organ, and that is our womb. When I said earlier that I had talked to all my organs but one during a Vipassana retreat, it was my womb that I had forgotten. The most distinctly feminine organ in my body, I had easily overlooked. It was a bit of a shock when I realized that later on, but not all that bizarre seeing how little we have been guided in developing our femininity from a feminine perspective. I had never ever had a talk about my womb or the powers it held, let alone a talk about the wounds of aggression against the feminine that needed healing. No, your womb would only come into play for your period and when pregnant. It was a forgotten organ, and as such its powers, with it the physical and energetic wounds were hidden too.

# Life and death

When I looked into this extraordinary organ, I found out that the womb is capable of creating DMT, something people look for via drugs. You can easily connect the dots and trace what these people are looking for. Surely they are right in knowing that the tensed natural way of Western society is not the one that created heaven on earth. When a baby is developed in uterus it goes through the altering energies of tension and relaxation, the tension being the moment of growth and relaxation the moment of integration. A baby naturally receives DMT to make the growth phases as gentle as possible. Hence our natural state in uterus is more like a meditative state, one that you are conditioned out of in Western society. But when you learn to release your conditionings profoundly, you do no longer need external sources of DMT to reach that gentle meditative state again, you can train your neurotransmitters back to making it yourself and feel all zen.

Dolphins can help you with this, their energy and sonar reach deep into your system. In Greek 'womb' means 'delphys', and 'delphin', 'dolphin' coming from the same root, somehow these magnificent creatures have a way of making you feel as in uterus again. Lots of research is being done on these animals and it is astounding what they have taught us so far. Professor in Business Ethics Thomas White writes in 'In defense of dolphins: The new moral frontier' how dolphin brains are structured with three times as many spindle cells as humans, the nerve cells responsible for being aware of another person's feelings and expressing empathy. The fact that they can use their sonar to scan bodies for temperature fluctuations, which indicates changing emotions, makes them function practically like an MRI scanner. Researchers Lilly and colleagues found that every breath of theirs is a conscious act, whereas we breathe automatically, meaning that they have more of their behavior under conscious control. In dolphin research other scientific words come in like resonance, entrainment, electromagnetic fields, ultrasound, sonochemistry and sonoluminescence and even DNA influencing via acoustic control. It is tremendous how cetaceans' senses are so much faster and broader in bandwidth than ours. Their acoustic system can bring in about forty times more data and about ten times more frequency ranges. Thus, communication with dolphins can best be described as telepathic or telempathic. When I went swimming with wild dolphins for a week, every day I asked for an insight to support my further development into womanhood. One day I had asked them to show me how to find more joy in the process. When somewhere that morning, two dolphins attracted my attention. I had wished for an intimate moment where I would be alone with the dolphins, and so I followed them when they swam away from the pod. I felt safe. It was so touching to see how that male and female graciously swam together, peacefully enjoying themselves together swimming all around me, back and forth. I started crying, feeling their state of happiness and peace in their bond, all light, free and joyous, making me realize I still had not yet reached such happiness again and was still deeply yearning for that feeling. After several years, even having started a new relationship, I suddenly felt the depth of the sadness again for having had to walk away from a relationship in which I had felt such a loving and blissful bond, although naïve and with a big undercurrent that sometimes popped up. I asked how to get back into that light state of love and fun in a relationship again. And the message I got was that I had to weep as deep as the highs of the joy I had lived. It is not easy to cry under water, but that day I cried more of the utterly deep tears that were still in my heart. I felt protected, supported and nourished with the dolphins' love and trust, there was an equally free space for my tears to stream and for my heart to blossom again. When I took a card from a dolphin tarot deck later that day, it read 'Protection' and indeed I had felt and still, most days, feel deeply protected by the universe. I got my next gift for feeling safe and sound the very next day. In the morning I had drawn the card 'Playfulness', and in that afternoon we found ourselves surrounded by and played with over one hundred curious playful quirking dolphins, what a joy! That entire week, you witnessed every single person gaining more and more of their childlike joyous and peaceful shimmer in their eyes again, returning home all serenely.

The common lack of this serenity, of knowing and feeling our uterus however has much to do with the Western behavior towards life's counterpart, death too. The powers of the uterus, of the life creating forces have been forgotten, just like its polar powers, the so closely related powers hidden in the word 'tomb'. Many women hold many tensions in their womb, for many it is a source of monthly pain and when gone through abortion, few have been capable to go through it without trauma. But that is only a consequence of not being educated how to treat it with the energy it requires to be vibrant and of support to your life. The more you know about death, the more you learn about life, the more you learn about the cycle.

I still have much to learn about the mysteries of the womb,

but I have been able to intuitively grasp some, namely those that have to do with the life-death-life cycle. I have once ended a pregnancy, like one third of all women. I thought I knew my body at that time, which clearly was not the case as I was still very much in the dark of how fertility of a woman works. Despite the moment of conception being of Utter Beauty, of being allowed to touch and take universal energy, I could easily feel from the first intuitive thought of the pregnancy that it was meant for a short visit only. No one involved was ready for a family yet and still had much to learn. I found out that I did not feel respected. That I was not yet there to fulfill my dream of conceiving in a pure loving relationship. Had the relationship, or better still I, have found balance already at that time, it would have been a whole different story. But lucky enough, when I called one of my friends, she was in that moment at a congress of gynecologists. So she could give me all the necessary information as to whether my body and fertility could get harmed by an abortion or not. With the well-developed procedures in the West, there was no physical limitation, which gave me the freedom to follow my heart and intuition. I had vowed many years before that I would be the most beautiful mother I could be for my children. But I had not settled in that woman yet, I was still looking for respect for my womanhood, my masculinity and their bond. As I had been confronted with women abusing their creative powers for babies out of manipulation instead of love, and having a way of blurting out hidden truths, I was not that surprised life gave me another experience to break open yet another feminine taboo. Which are the cause of many unnecessary tensions between men and women.

The strange part is that in that same week I had been reading for the first time about the life-death-life cycle as a feminine responsibility. And there I found myself, immediately having to put it into practice. I had already had many past life experiences. Whether this is personal or universal information signaling about life, it is a commonality when you reach a certain level of meditation. And I had been granted a touch of universal energy, from which everything comes and everything returns to. I knew about the cycle by energetic experience but I had never lived it in the flesh. So I took on my life lesson and to honour all the energies involved, I said I would listen to why this pregnancy happened the way it did. I quickly came to learn that I had no examples of conception of a pure nature around me, no one was aware of the cycle of life-death-life when conceiving a baby. Several times I had meditative experiences that had to do with losing a baby and I learned that globally too many women are still scandalized for being a sexual human being, for becoming pregnant outside the restricted confines of a society's norms. When a woman's capacity to conceive is dishonoured from the very first moment, it traumatizes her. When a woman cannot fall back on healthy bonding and support in her family or society, how can she bond healthily with her child then, how can she teach it to feel safe and nurtured when she herself is not so? Add to these overwhelming feelings the global numbers of sexual and emotional abuse, rape, teenage brides, women dying during child birth and women not being mistress of their own bodies, I cried tons. Having cried all the tears, I realized then that if I wanted to heal myself to my core, the only way for me, was to heal my uterus by the activation of her capacity and imprints.

I was blessed with remarkably noble women who make it their life work to guide other women, having created a place to carry other women in their most vulnerable state. Just like gynecologists will save a mother's life before that of the baby, these women I met had a refined wisdom and honour for life. They were very aware of the difference between the responsibility for giving life and giving a life of quality. They made me see the powerlessness of a man in such a situation, in these days maybe one of the few for a man, and that the final choice lay with the woman. In following a meditative experience of losing a baby, years before, I had read a touching book of Walter Makichen about the souls of babies. It was one of those books standing in the store waiting for you to bring it home. It stated about abortion that sometimes souls come to learn something specific only. Something they can only learn through these two people in that specific moment in time and that specific situation. The generosity of life. They then wait where newborn souls reside for their parents to get ready for the next part of their joint journey. Yet others choose another couple since they learned what they could with the first chosen couple. Therefore when you open up to your intuitions and connect to a baby's soul, to listen to and learn this energy's gifts of wisdom and growth, it may be a soothing and life-altering experience.

It is weird and wonderful to say but the day of the expulsion was magnificently stunning. My ex-partner was with me. In that moment he enveloped me in loving energy. He made love to me energetically, and the energetic waves my uterus received by that must have been an extra support for the ease of the expulsion, I could hardly believe that there had been no pain involved. A little later we went for a walk in the sunshine and drank tea on a terrace. And then suddenly, an energy came over me, a veil of such an otherworldly sweetness, like an angel touching me. For an hour long, I could barely open my eyes, I was high on the sweetest energy. My companion smiling deeply in awe as he could see and feel something extraordinary was happening to me. I knew by this sweetest gift that I had honoured the baby's soul journey.

# Surrendering to cosmic love

It would be only two years later when I read about the astronaut Edgar Mitchell's oneness experience in space that I recognized the same vibration. The astronaut speaks about having lived a connection between his molecules and the ones of the stars he was surrounded by in deep space. He had just come to learn at Harvard and MIT that we are indeed made up of the same molecules as the stars. So he could easily grasp what was happening. He described his experience as 'a feeling of ecstasy and wellbeing that submerged me completely, a feeling of being one with the universe, a bubblicious joy, a feeling of happiness and awakening'. He had looked in many places to understand what had happened, researching scientific literature and religious literature of all different traditions, until some university scholars talked to him about the Sanskrit state 'Savikalpa Samadhi'. A state, he further learned, was common among shamans, wizards, medicine men and holders of different spiritual traditions too. Such an extraordinary experience is so profound and often deeply transformative. Like Edgar Mitchell said, 'We left as technicians and came back as humanists'. Such extraordinary experiences are often termed supernatural, often have a form that is hardly common, and are often seen as incomprehensible by the viewpoint of current scientific knowledge. And although such experiences fall out of the norm, they are real and form a true challenge for the spirit of every scientist.

For sure there are less intense ways to heal your uterus from your lifestyle, ancestral lineage, false beliefs about yourself and our collective heritage. There are several massage forms that help you restore it. All internal energetic balancing body therapies do that. The most potent one is a tantric massage when done in the true tantric loving way by a truly loving person, you can sense their heart from a distance. Tantra is the art of complete surrender, of letting go to love, we all can use help with that. A less intimate way is a Mayan abdominal massage that can be self taught. It relaxes the muscles and ligaments and puts the uterus back in its place. Apparently ninety percent have at one point or the other a misplaced uterus causing much discomforts.

Unfortunately these days there are many women who are unaware of the role of their uterus. Sterilization is offered as a healthy common practice, a procedure often done after having the desired number of babies, bringing it back to a pure material function for babies only. You should understand that we do not, as Newton once said, work like a clockwork where you can easily change the parts. Once that might have been an insight in our progression, but it is the same as still saying that the earth is flat. Such actions do influence your entire energy flow. It is the same in the animal kingdom, with the most obvious example clipping a stallion, the entire character of the horse changes. Nevertheless it is not so that when you have a hysterectomy, you loose all your femininity and capacity for creation. It will influence you profoundly, but yet again, it is how you deal with it energetically. The Mayan massage cures many ailments that often follow such a surgery and can help you to restore balance. To give you a comparison, there is an American little girl with only one brain hemisphere, nonetheless she has developed the functions the other side is responsible for. So it is not about the physical form but about the plasticity of it, the changeable and energetic form. Doctors Deepak Chopra and Rudy Tanzi dispell in their book 'Super brain' the five brain myths we are used to following, being 'the injured brain cannot heal itself, the brain's hardwiring cannot be changed, aging in the brain is inevitable and irreversible, the brain loses millions of cells a day that cannot be replaced, and primitive reactions like fear and aggression overrule the higher brain'. This is quantum science being incorporated in medicine. As with the brain, the same goes for our organs that make up our feminine nature.

So it is important that you question what you were taught to be true about your uterus and what feels right for you. It is a matter of questioning your body and hence also your erotic nature. It is about questioning how you as a woman live and feel joy from within. If you would learn that your orgasm comes from the contractions your uterus makes, I am sure you would be inspired to dig a little deeper. When, on top of that, I tell you that the same muscles of your uterus are responsible for a painful or an orgasmic birth of a baby, I am sure you will heighten your attention and self-care. Have you ever considered that giving birth with pain may be a limited, outdated view of one of the most natural acts? That it is but a natural consequence of the triangle fear, tension and pain? There is a logic in all of nature, why then would a woman's body go against it? What would happen if every woman decides to let go of all the old pains and liberate herself from her core to restore her body, and spirit?

*Nature knows the big secret*
*and smiles.*
Victor Hugo

# CHAPTER 3

# Body Food

We are what we eat, and so the basic rule goes, keep good food in and poisonous food out. On all levels, from the physical, emotional, mental to the spiritual as they all influence your body and mind. We feed ourselves with all our senses, so also with our eyes and ears, hence it is important to stand still at what that means for each of us personally. Children have a natural intelligence to know what is good for them and what not, yet they are often trained out of it or not listened to, leading to a distortion of their innate wisdom. When you are trained into sort of liking what you dis-like, you slowly get further and further away from your inner voice that knows exactly what goes with you and what not, what gives you energy and what detracts energy. And so you might have to learn the discernment between good and poisonous food for you again. In a system that trained you for the rigid norm of the zeitgeist of patriarchy, what maybe two percent of the people truly corresponded to, you were not trained to be yourself but someone else. How I have wished on my journey, for a system that supports one in finding our unique place naturally, a place that makes you believe in the sanctity of life. As a young woman I chose to fit myself, not the norm anymore. Why would I even want to fit the norm of the end of a patriarchal era which is extremely neurotic and all but happy, balanced, open and wise? And how then, would I have to learn to not put my situation up as the norm for others?

If we are all fed and conditioned in the same manner, away from our authenticity, our true self that feels secure, accepted and at peace, in the case of the two percent, you would then get ninety-eight percent of people who have low self-esteem. However you need a strong sense of self not to internalize someone else's doubts and stand up for your unique nature, refraining from subordination. The consequence is that when living our authenticity is not seen as our highest contribution to the world, we naturally go and compensate actively and compensation and a false self become built-in commodities, leading to stress, doubt and insecurity. On the positive side, since we are group creatures that need bonding and social contact, this makes it easy to then relate to almost the entire human population's inner world, whether they are aware of having been trained out of their true core or not. If you felt alone, you no longer are, and you may come to realize that you find yourself alone together with many others. This makes you ready to understand and integrate the true meaning and reason for being alone. You can connect again from within. Then you can become happily alone, all-one. The only requirement for living that experience, is that you open up to be vulnerable, bringing all aspects of you into one, into your consciousness, that makes the deeply unique and wonderful creature that is you. It is only you who can do that. You can receive support and aid to grow in a safe surrounding of course, but the essential work is done by yourself. Just like the saying goes, 'You can walk with someone, but no one can walk your path for you'.

So you are to learn what suits you and what does not. On all levels, food, clothes, friends, lovers, theories, work, lifestyle, sports, hobbies, emotional behavior, cultural belief systems, spiritual development, everything. You might be surprised by the difference between your conditioned self and your true self. Sometimes it is pure joy, and sometimes it is pure misery, the levels will vary of how conscious you were when you swallowed your food and how much you ate. You can learn how every aspect of life feels inside of you, whether it is comfortable or uncomfortable, whatever is necessary to let go of the old and bring in the new, the true you that has always been waiting there for you. Once you can grasp that your difficulties in life are also your gifts of life, that both feeling good and feeling bad are essential parts of each of us, showing us the way, then your wisdom will help to make room for you. It is just up to you to pick it up, dust it off and shine again.

# Physical food

So let us start with the physical food. Children's taste buds develop in stages, first their sweet buds are activated, then they can discover sharp tastes, followed by salty, sour and bitter tastes. Imagine that you were supported as a child in learning your own taste preferences, that with every specific taste you were offered a whole range of new savory experiences, discovering the subtle differences within one array of taste and being allowed to choose your favourites. And when you were ready for a whole new set of tastes, when ready to discover the tastes of bitterness, it was mingled for you with something you already really liked. You were supported in gently and naturally stretching a capacity, as that is what is growing. In this way you would have been properly taught to develop your own capacity for discernment and trusting your own preferences from an early age on, it would have been the most natural thing. When you are taught to trust your inner experiences, your trust in yourself and so your trust in your discernment for what is good for you and what not in the outer world, you become solid like a rock, capable of walking your own path healthily, joyously and faithfully.

## Habits and beliefs

If you did not properly develop these skills, with life sometimes leaving you very confused, showing you missed some parts, you can easily start the discovery for your true self with your food. The quality of your food is highly essential for a vibrant body of course, a good energy flow and accompanying soul. Since all is about balance, and our bodies these days are pretty acidic because of Western diet, you do yourself a big favor by paying attention to alkalize your system. If you would eat whole foods and let your body grab the vegetables it gravitates to, it would actually naturally balance itself out. But most people follow a mainstream Western diet that is very acidic, leading to acidification of your body, a huge source of many diseases. Sometimes this acidification does not even show in blood tests as it has followed a deeper course and nestled itself in the cells. If you knew how one glass of a coke can severely drop your pH-level, obligating your system to find the alkaline energy elsewhere in your body to balance your pH again, you would quickly stop drinking it like water.

Another cause of acidification is that Western diet also consists of a lot of animal foods. Eating animal foods is a regional phenomenon, whereas two third of other food cultures in the world are of a vegetarian or vegan nature. The documentary 'Forks over knives' documents how many studies have been done and show how cancers are not a worldwide phenomenon but are directly linked to the type of diet people consume. If you are very much pro eating meat stating that people have always eaten meat in certain regions, it is important to take into account that animals used to have a very different lifestyle and constitution compared to our current livestock. Instead of running freely, these days many animals are caged without movement, often fed with carcinogenous food and overfed in a very short period of time, not even receiving the time to develop their paws to carry their own body weight. Such meat is watery instead of rich, and no longer that nutritious. Add to that the way animals are killed these days, and you feed yourself their stress hormones on top of the ones you already have. But we have come so used to eating meat that we rarely question these methods anymore. People often believe they need meat for strength because their body starts to tremble after a couple of days without it, but this is actually your body showing the addiction you have created for your body. You definitely need protein of course but thinking you need it from meat is just one of the many tales created by industry corporates. Like the story that created the belief you need milk every day for your calcium intake and strong bones, which unfortunately is not true as dairy is also very acidifying. The strongest effects of stories creating false beliefs I witnessed in Zacatecas, a village in Mexico. Its people believe that the soft drink cola cures them from all ailments, that you burp them out. Talking about a company that once had very good yet unethical sales men. Just like the ones that sold alcohol there, installing a tradition in the village that people came to believe that with carnival they could cleanse their livers by drinking alcohol for thirty days. Such irresponsible activities led to a village having an average death rate age of forty years now because their livers can no longer cope with their bodies' acidification.

But not only our livers are attacked by an acidic diet, our pineal glands are also affected. This master gland can get calcified purely by the diet you eat. Calcification means that it is closed for its proper functioning. The pineal gland is the first gland to be formed in the fetus and is activated and visible after seven weeks after conception. It is also at the end of these seven weeks, on day forty-nine that we sexually diversify, meaning that an embryo becomes a boy or a girl. This gland controls the various bio-rhythms in our body and as such is very sensitive to light. Needless to say that there is more to it than just a very vital physical function.

Its importance is known in various teachings from all over the world. In Eastern teachings this gland corresponds to the sixth and seventh chakra of their energy system teachings, and in the West the French philosopher René Descartes who was actually the founder of the rational worldview, stated it to be the seat of the soul. It is seen as your inner eye, and is in fact composed of the same material as the physical eye, the cornea and retina. This gland is so significant, that it is seen as the temple of the human body, the holy of holiest. It is the Coeur as architecturally laid out in our churches, there where the light is the strongest, where the priests commune directly with God and convey their words to the lay men. The importance of this gland is also traceable back to Tibetan culture. It is remarkable that they say that on day forty-nine the soul of a recently deceased person enters a new incarnation, exactly corresponding to the seven weeks when the pineal is activated and a fetus takes on its gender. Even Christianity conveys these teachings, just told a little differently. It marks this day as the day the Holy Spirit came over the disciples so that they themselves would understand his teachings directly, Pentecost is the fiftieth day of Easter. So on day forty-nine the story goes 'That the elders in the temple were surprised by a gusting wind when suddenly tongues of fire came down and rested upon their heads'. This symbolically means that their crown chakra, the seventh chakra corresponding to their pineal gland, became illuminated and fully functional, the spirit came down onto man.

In Taoist culture the pineal gland is part of a portion of the brain they call 'the Crystal Palace'. In ancient Egyptian culture this is portrayed by the 'Eye of Ra' and in esoteric Christianity, the Christian mystic tradition it is called 'the Vaulted Chamber of initiation', around which sit three kings, the pineal being one of these kings. So the pineal gland is utterly essential in connecting heaven and earth, it is the very key to the highest and most divine consciousness in man. It is your cosmic antenna in your body and important in activating your soul and your higher powers to create heaven on earth. Analogically, as it is so sensitive to light, the more inner light, the more cosmic energy you can store in your body, the stronger your higher powers become and the easier it is to elevate yourself, your surroundings as well as the people around you. This all means that your diet can actually inhibit feeling a connection with Source, which is a very common ailment in the West. So inform yourself on what you eat, feel again what it does to you. Remember that knowledge and experience are power, we have the access to it in the West, it is waiting for you to decide to use it.

## Sustainable ways

Sustainable living is hence your best option to live and support your full potential. In every aspect of your life, you can co-lead the change to sustainable, healthy ways by the products you choose. Hence, inserting feminine principles in our companies is of essence too. Every industry has its own path in evolving into sustainable balanced ways of course, but the speed of many industries adapting to human friendly ingredients often depend on their dependency on the chemical industry, which luckily is evolving too. Changing old ways requires time to do life cycle analysis, investigate new healthy ways, change supplier or production lines or work methods in general. But it is all there, companies and their people cannot pretend otherwise any longer and shove the change on to future generations. So these days it is no longer about capability, as all technological and managerial knowledge on doing business in sustainable ways is there. Neither is it too expensive when calculated on the long run. Especially not with externalities coming to the forefront, with companies carrying the costs they create for people's and nature's health themselves, costs which have long been heaved on to society via taxes. Now it is a matter of human and natural values. It is about correcting bad habits and supporting good ones. It is about offering services that nurture the life essence of the body, heart and soul. If you want to live in a healthier world, you help by supporting the ones who make the leap so you can live naturally. This is how change happens, not by keeping to the status quo and shedding responsibility on to others' shoulders, it is by you and I, by working together and supporting each other. If you add all the you's and I's in the world, you have an incredible amount of power. You can choose how to use it, I use it for a natural, healthy, happy and soulful way of living, feeding my body and the cycles of nature the most natural products.

I started at the bottom with changing my Western diet to a sustainable diet, quite surprised how unhealthy Western diet actually is. Sustainable foods have the characteristics of no additives, which will require you to read the labels again when you go shopping in your supermarket. However, your regular supermarket with its regular foods contains tons of additives, practically all synthetic, often carcinogenic. It is the old way the chemical industry makes a lot of money together with the food industry. I was quite astonished to see what is labeled as food these days. If you choose nutritious, wholesome food for yourself and your body however you may be obliged to switch supermarket. Sustainable foods are free from radiation too, which takes out the nutrients as well, they are free from toxic sprayed products, are free from infection by their genetically modified organisms and they grow on nutrient soil. Nutrient soil is not possible with agricultural methods of monoculture, big industry's way to make its profits bigger every time, and depleted soil gives less nutritive harvests. Also the water that flows in the region where you eat your fruits and vegetables from, has an effect as some streams have become polluted, also in the West. If you find sustainable foods to be more expensive than regular foods, look at it in the long term, as an investment in your health which will definitely pay off. Or go and shop directly at the farmers' market. It is fun to have that contact again, see their passion for the food they produce. When you buy local produce, costs will be lower as there are no shipping costs and chances of radiation to ensure the foods reach their destination edible are lowered too. Nevertheless prices are lowering as these products are slowly becoming the mainstream. It is a natural consequence of people becoming more conscious and preventative as they see so many people getting sick. I know it can be uncomfortable to be confronted with the current state of such a basic thing as the health of our food, which you would expect to be healthy no matter what, but unfortunately it is our reality these days. Luckily here in the West we have other options these days too. When you choose wholesome foods you discover new tastes and your body and mind will love it and flourish, 'Let thy food be thy medicine and thy medicine be thy food.'

Besides knowing where my food came from, I shockingly got into cooking too. I learned that cooking my own food helps me to ground deeply. It helps to make contact to your body again and learn to feel again what it needs. You become aware of nature again, you may even find yourself being drawn to enter it again. Even your taste buds will take on their initial quality once more when you eat naturally again. The idea of cooking may put you off with your busy schedule, but cooking does not necessarily require much time, especially not if you eat vegetarian or vegan. I am a queen at cooking the easy way, yet it supports me in slowing down. If you do find it hard to make time for nurturing yourself by yourself, you can make bigger portions and freeze them. Enjoying your own care daily again starts with the small, practical daily things.

Taking it one step further, the rule of only taking good stuff in also applies to anything you put on your body, as via your skin the ingredients get into your bloodstream too. Make-up and hygiene are bodily foods. A coroner once said that during his career he learned that if he were allowed to prohibit one thing, it would be make-up as the livers of the women he treated were so often filled with goo and glitter. Everything that is foreign to your body or nature gives your liver problems, which makes you age quicker and get sick much quicker. So if or when you use make-up and hygienic products, look for natural lines. More and more brands are bringing them on the market. This goes for deodorants too, women need to pay extra attention to the deodorant they use as yet again the ingredients can influence and clog the lymph system and enhance breast cancer. Again, the rule goes and go for the most natural you can find. Which may even go for clothes. You might be surprised but also your clothes have an effect on your body. The fabrics you wear will open or close your pores more than the other. Truly everything has an effect on your body.

And so within as without. Pay attention to the products you use to clean your house, your car and any other appliances. What you put into the water, is what you feed nature and since nature feeds you, it is what you feed yourself ultimately. So many people use toxic cleaning materials, and it is the sum of all that makes us pay so many taxes on health or public services like clean water, with clean still being very relative, even in industrialized countries, as the systems do not filter everything yet. It is all the small things together, like the pesticide on your apple, your detergent via your skin, the toxic particles in the air and so on that make for one unhappy liver. Luckily all is in development, and every time you can, try to go for the newest standards in ecomaterial. Read people's work, people who researched how to create a toxic-free home for yourself and your children. The thought alone of contributing to a lighter and happier world, for yourself and the ones you love, when buying and using these is already worth while. You feel yourself officially uplifted from cavemen consciousness contributing to a whole new world, open to sensitivity and true care again.

# Energy in motion food

With emotional food the same rule applies of keeping poisonous food out and good food in. It is exactly the same, just at a more subtle level. It is wonderful and invigorating to have feasts of positive emotions, they make you strong and radiant. However, when people try to feed you poisonous emotions, try to hold your mouth closed or spit it out, preferably instantly without hesitation if you have reached that state of discernment, of what is nutritious for you and what is not, who and what you are or are not. So do not hold back because you were taught to be pretty and silent. Maybe switch journals or channels and feed yourself positive news. Keeping negative influences out, requires simultaneously creating a distance between you and others while yet connecting. As said before, people project their old stories onto the ones around them in an attempt to find their way home. Home as in living your true nature. But not all people are equally interested in the Truth or find themselves at the same stop along the road, some even want you to stay at their stop and do anything to prevent you from going your own way. That can make it hard sometimes, but when you recognize that everybody is exactly at the level from where they can grow, it becomes a little easier. You cannot teach a first grader the teaching material of a fifth grader, it would not be supportive. And similarly, there will be people cheering you on. Arthur Schopenhauer once beautifully said, 'All truth passes through three stages. First, it is ridiculed. Second, it is violently opposed. Third, it is accepted as self-evident'. Just like the earth was once seen as flat and now correctly as round, emotions have been walking a similar path. They have to do with the past, and leaving the past behind, healthily, integrated. They are the link between your spirit and your body. When you master their innate intelligence you can improve that link and read both of them better.

## Digesting personal messages

When your emotions fluctuate inside of you and take you off centre, they alert you and help you to see what is moving inside of you from the past, what you are still to learn to get back to centre. The key is to observe yourself and keep breathing. It is of essence not to identify anybody with the emotions. An emotion is something you experience, not what you are. If you want to identify yourself to something however, do it to love, true all conveying love that dares to see things for what they are and has the courage to deal with them. True love is the only constant in life, even if you cannot yet touch upon it. Your emotions however come and go. You just learn to apply to emotions the cycle of life-death-life, feel them, live them, surrender to them, give them all the space they need to just be – without harming another, without any judgment, observe their movements as it were and follow them till the end, where they die and can be reborn to show you their gift. With practice, it can go from emotions lasting a lifetime, to emotions lasting a second.

To make it easy, 'The liberating power of emotions' explains that there are four basic emotions, fear, anger, sadness and happiness, all the others, like insecurity, distrust, resentment, jealousy, depression, despair, minimal living and seriousness are a consequence of pent-up basic emotions. Key is to make them flow again, and in that way transform the negative emotions into positive ones, like courage, trust, sincerity, identity, vitality, joy, gratitude and playfulness. Flow is about letting go of the end result of your actions, of not being attached and not being upset when you need to change your ways to optimize your situation. It helps to make your second chakra, your pelvic area healthy, as it is the balancing place for your emotions and makes going through your emotions lighter, you will not attach more importance to them then what they are here to teach you. So it is about being able to make the proper translation of every e-motion and be a watchful student.

If you follow an emotion to its root, you will always find love at the end. You might have to go through some pain first, but well expressed emotions are a source of more love. But this does not necessarily mean people are easily stimulated to go through the natural emotional process. Because choosing for love, in our day and age still means having to go through the experiences of absence of love and that can be quite terrifying depending on what you have experienced. In such a situation it comes in handy when you know what emotions want to tell you. Sadness and depression evoke an awareness and articulation of, often old, repressed thoughts and emotions that otherwise stay hidden behind lighter and more cheerful moods. It may teach you how to let go of old dying beliefs and may make you wiser if you are open to integrate it. Anger is not the primary sin as some people in power wanted you to believe. Anger is just an energy, and when you cut of your anger, you cut of your energy which makes you weak. Christian Pankhurst describes beautifully why anger is so essential, 'Without it, it can leave you merging with others, being bipolar, depressed, numb, co-dependent, addicted, losing your boundaries, decreasing your magnetism, your radiance and your sexual presence'. He also explains that when anger comes from you feeling unworthy, it shows as rage, but from a worthy source it shows healthy and kindly. Just like gossip and blasphemy are strong expressions of unworthiness and anger too. So you definitely want to use it and learn to transform it, just like an alchemical process and use the energy for its original purpose. One of its purposes is to set your boundaries, to protect or develop what is dear to you, to correct the wrong, or to show you that your essence has been violated. Do you see it as bad when a lioness hisses and growls when protecting her cubs? A lioness knows how to use this strength naturally and healthily, we women are taught out of it. When not dealt with properly, anger can even turn against you and show its face as aggression, within your body too. When frustrations keep building up, which come from things perceivably going against your will, you might find yourself becoming aggressive, having a shorter fuse than normally. Your anger has then become destructive instead of constructive. Anger shows you that you need to improve things in your life, that there is more about yourself to learn and room for growth. Aggression then is common in a culture that strengthens your will for action and not your natural talents, which develop more smoothly. These loads of hidden frustration show themselves in many ways, are easily spotted in traffic, in the overload of young female nudity in the media and via our children who act out the wrongs of our society. Staying angry at another means you actually do not want to deal with the mirrored part of yourself. But if you can be grateful for the initial situation, you can transform the frustrations, and when operating more from alignment instead of will, it becomes an interesting story. Women carry much natural power, a source they can tap into if they shed the patriarchal belief that a woman should be only sweet and silent. What would happen if you would no longer feed yourself with the cultural straitjacket you have lived? Do you become afraid? Do you feel standing strong or more like being on drift sand, no longer knowing who you then are? In all, everything is about solving your relationship to your own power. From that perspective, an identity crisis can then actually be a great gift. It shows you that you need to step up spiritually and learn to deal with the point of transformation you have reached from a higher perspective than you used before.

In such a situation it helps if you know what fear asks of you, what message it holds for you. Fear is a naturally built in system to protect us from physical harm. But in the Western world people still activate their fear even when there is no actual threat, there are no wild animals and they have enough food and a roof above their heads. But threats can easily be created to instill fear, fear as a food, is the easiest way to subordinate people. The meeker people are, the easier they will surrender to your power and not question your actions. It is the best way to disempower people as they easily offer their power to a so called stronger force. For sure it is a tactic that is not only practiced in the West. The people of the Middle East have shown beautifully in the Arab Spring what fear can bring you to if you follow it to its essence. It is a way for you to develop courage. Like Marianne Williamson's quote, 'Our deepest fear is not that we are inadequate. Our deepest fear is that we are powerful beyond measure. It is our light, not our darkness that most frightens us'. Just like love is the opposite of hate, fear is the opposite of courage. It is the same energy, but in another degree, it is the transformed aspect of an emotion. If you dissect the word courage, you come to the French 'coeur-age', the age of the heart. My loyalty is to that, to love, to truth, that is my power and that is what makes me, as gently and powerfully as possible, move through the places where love or truth are not present in me yet. It can be quite challenging, but in every moment I have the choice to set my mind to being pulled by the vision I hold in my heart.

# Happy food

When you know how to let go of the negative ones to make room for a life of love and fun, what do you want to eat as emotional food then? You want positive, energizing feelings like ease, care, appreciation, forgiveness, gratitude, compassion, vitality and joy. It is exactly these that define a state of flow, where everything happens with effortless effort. It is a most wonderful state to live life in. Contrary to depleting emotions, the Heart Math Institute found that renewing emotions establish hormonal balance, build resilience, cause system-wide coherence, improve your mental clarity, and in all optimize your performance, simply by focusing on inner solutions instead of external ones. It is allowing emotions that got unnaturally fixed to flow again into their essence, like going from a pool to a flowing current that finds its way home to the ocean. You can start by identifying what makes you happy, what makes your heart tingle and your eyes shine bright. You can make a treasure chest and fill it with all reminders of deep joy, songs, pictures, words, letters, memories, perfume, reminders of activities that lift you up, and dive into it when you feel you are going down or below zero emotionally. This is divine food, exactly to your taste, use it, you are the only one who can make it exactly to your liking. Every day you have the personal choice how you want to feel that day. The more great food you give yourself, the more and longer you will live in flow. There you are at your best. Physically, emotionally, mentally and spiritually, energizing feelings are key to a happy life.

Wisdom teachings know this, and hence they have meditations to generate compassion, which is like the sum of many positive emotions. Richard Davidson is a neuroscientist who researches the effect of meditation on the brain and works with Buddhist monks. Tibetan monks train in compassion meditation by which they enter gamma waves, deep brain waves you can measure. This meditation has the capacity to alter emotions. It activates a zone in the left prefrontal cortex where positive emotions are seated and helps to connect to other parts in the brain that are connected to empathy. This training strengthens the likelihood of spontaneously entering states of compassion when confronted with suffering in the external world. It even alters conditioned neuronal circuits in your brain, meaning that your conditioned basic emotional state can be transformed, and so your behavior. It enhances your social intuition, it becomes easier to recognize the needs of and the good in others and that they too, are just searching for happiness. More gifted brains like Richard are researching the area of compassion at the Greater Good Science Center at the University of California.

It has been known for ages that healthy emotional balance can also be reached through drama, theater and other creative outlets. It was once seen as a spiritual endeavor for the few, not as mere entertainment. Four thousand years ago Bharat Muni advised kings to partake in drama and theater to consciously learn and live through emotions that were not part of their daily lives. Artistic expression ignites the potential joy within yourself, it is just a matter of finding your expression form. A long time ago in India, economy was even built upon artistic contributions that found their base in the spiritual plane. This of course, is distinctly different than merely creating art for the sake of outbursts of emotion. If you use art consciously it can have a cathartic effect and change you profoundly. Recently Professor of Psychology, Dacher Keltner found that awe, the feeling of being in the presence of something vastly greater than yourself, that exceeds your current knowledge structures has been found to break up people's routine and challenge themselves to think in new ways. Positive emotions open up your mind.

## Levels of relationship

The beauty of it all is that emotions will always pop up when you have fallen out of these beautiful positive states. And they can similarly bring you back into it, that is their amazing food for you if you know how to digest it. And when you have digested them all, you become deeply satisfied and strong and your communication can yet again become a gift of renewing emotions. The most basic thing you are to digest to live this is the image you were fed of a man and a woman. And the collective image Western society created about a man and a woman is not particularly the most loving or balanced one. Everyone learns by imitation, so you are actually fed the image of a woman by your mother primarily, whether present or not. And similarly by the example your father set and the one society set. Your parents define your definition of a man and a woman. Even if you think you are very different, you might one day find yourself actually living the same relationship as your parents, unless you were brought up to consciously create your own definition of a man, a woman and a loving relationship between the two. Hence you were also fed your definition of the inner girl, inner boy, woman and man, the nurturing energy of a mother and the protective energy of a father, or the lack thereof, and consequently your definition of love and unity in a relationship, with yourself and with others.

There are different levels of love in a relationship, influenced by the level of independence. Wayne Dyer highlights the difference between relationships characterized by dependence or independence. In dependent relationships the commitment is motivated by deficiency, there is a mutual agreement to offer what each needs. Love is not for free here, and so you may also be confronted with a thing called love as a manipulation method. Despite the big word of independence that we so often use in the West, you can easily see nonetheless that the Western relationship average is still characterized by high dependence, a natural trait of patriarchal relationships. I understand it actually finds its origin in the Western concept of God. If you unconsciously still hold an image that God created man in sin, why then would you deserve a truly loving relationship and a bountiful life? If you hold the image of God as only loving you when you behave in a certain way, you step into a realm of conditional loving. In such a relationship there is no freedom to be you, there is no motivation to share your inner richness, nor the possibility to make yourself happy, as you will always depend on the conditions of someone else. The universe does not judge or moralize, it is we that do this out of emotionally non-resolved themes. Similarly if you hold the concept that God is a man, then you are surely in for inferior feeling as a woman, no balanced relationships can come out of that. And if you see God as being the savior as in you being at his mercy without any will power or a voice of your own, you are in for a disempowering relationship. Rescuer-ship, both in its active and its passive form, holds no empowerment for neither of the parties involved, companionship and support however tell a very different story. When you believe you cannot evolve into love yourself, surrendering to the help of another can create miracles. Need satisfaction wants to hold on, love on the other hand lets go. When you take the concept of God for Love, then every relationship offers a means to find your way back into love.

Luckily you can grow into true independent and free relationships, where motivated by sharing your authentic self. But for that of course, you need to know your true self first. Such relationships are about recognizing each other's soul program, playing fair, taking responsibility for your own heritage and supporting each other's dying wish to realize one's heart's desire. You know that you alone are responsible for getting your true self out there and connect freely. From there you can experience feelings of oneness, while being distinctly yourself and different, with everything being out in the open. This is not a fluffy experience, there is no fluffy, weak love here that hovers over everything, it is very grounded, deeply honest and deeply human. But the road thereto will show you everything that is not yet unified, so here you get a true master class of balancing masculine and feminine energies, of all poles in life. True love is recognized by its gifts of guiding you to know your core, through all the accumulated dirt, right up to your deepest part, the most inspiring part that is you. It is your free choice to choose on which level you want to live your relationships. But whatever the relationship, it will bring you to wholeness only if you chose to open your eyes. Every event, whether beautiful or painful, is really an invitation to go to a higher and deeper level of relationship, with yourself and another. The fullness of Love is an achievable goal for any human being.

## True colours

The food you were brought up with however, is the one you will keep wanting until you break the cycle and consciously see and feel where you are. Until that time you will keep feeding yourself the same food from your childhood, this time voluntarily by the men and women you attract into your life. As a woman you actually project the image of a man that you were fed by your father, male siblings and society, onto your partner, or you attract men that fit the image. This will keep repeating until you let it go and decide to create your own version, until you decide to let go of the past, learn its lessons and integrate and live their presents lovingly in the now. For this, it is essential that you learn to define yourself as emotionally separate from your environment. Only then can you truly unite again without losing yourself. When you go deeper and deeper into consciousness, you gain a more profound understanding that you created everything. Even if it looks as if someone else initiated an experience, there must have been a receiver to connect the experience to. It is what we mentally do with energies, with experiences, our program creates others behavior. When you can let go of a conservative mind-set and understand that the other person only triggers what is already inside you, or shows burdens that have not yet completely healed, or qualities you need to develop, you go a long way. So when you look at others, try to look into the mirror. Integrate your emotions with your intellect as it is not black and white mirroring, life is a bit more complex than that, but if you pay attention and are willing to look honestly at yourself, you can see what the other is teaching you. And instead of looking at what others create, if you want to compare, compare yourself more with yourself. Have you evolved in love and relationships, are you grounded more in your own true version, have you created more you?

So to feed yourself and your life with the man, or woman, that fits and feeds your heart's desire, it is easier to know first what the heart's desire of the woman is that you are. Her heart's desire, not her wish list for her wardrobe, nor those of friends or those that movie stars play for you. To answer your heart's call is the best food ever, and it is uniquely yours. You will feel the energy of the man that fits your womanhood like a glove, right there in the centre of your heart. And for that man to show up in your life, you will need to clean yourself emotionally from others' desires and images. When you stand by your own, you will attract a man that stands by his woman, in all circumstances. He might actually already be standing in front of you. But just as wearing blue coloured glasses colours your surroundings, not showing reality as it is, so does your emotional lens do. And his. Patriarchal definitions of a successful man and woman are changing rapidly, so it is the perfect time to jump on the wagon, and choose your lens to allow whatever needs to happen, whatever time, support and love it requires.

# Soul food

For many Westerners the concept of soul is a very abstract thing. With a worldview that sees things as unanimated that is not a surprise. Belief is often seen as something for the uneducated. And in some way that is true, as believing is a quality of the right brain hemisphere, the hemisphere that has had hardly any training in the West. More so, we were even trained out of believing our firsthand experience or intuition by our current rationally-scientific schooling models. But let me ask you this, do you believe? Do you believe in yourself? Do you believe in your experience of beauty? Do you believe in your child? Do you believe in your congressmen? Do you believe that the sun will rise tomorrow, that the universe will keep our planet in its right course? At one point, a nun told me that believing in the Divine is a gift. And it is indeed, believing opens you up for the wondrous and miraculous in life, it is a gift that is right there to take, for everybody as you freely choose to reactivate it in your brain.

# A bridge

Contrary to the West, two thirds of the world population has a worldview that holds several realms of reality. Their view is much richer in spiritual development, showing how poor Western culture is in that field. Which as said before, was not always the case. Our shamans worked on the physical and the soul level, the soul being the connection between our material bodies and the cosmic realms. It is where you hold the purest version of yourself. It tells you what you came here for, what your purpose in life is and hence what gives you deepest fulfillment in life. A successful life is therefore about bringing soul into matter. Plato wrote about the soul that 'it lives on a subtle level yet can still hurt, that it is untouchable yet real, and that it is complex and yet comprehensible'.

Before having directly experienced it, the closest intuition most have about the soul, is that it resides in the heart. And our heart is indeed the bridge. It is the bridge between our lower chakras, which represent the earthy, and our higher ones, which represent the higher realms, our heart is our own shaman connecting the two. Living merely in the higher or the lower chakras holds no balance, nor real truth about life as a human being. There are many spiritual traditions that forsake the physical earthy aspect, that tell you to transcend your body, material things and emotions. And from Western history and many of its priests we know what the consequences can be of such a philosophy. Similarly, when you only live in the lower ones, and focus on matter and sex without the involvement of the heart and the higher energy fields, we also know from Western society what that has led to.

It is important to understand that it is indeed about transcendence, but as dualistic thinking Westerners we easily misinterpret the words of ancient texts. You can only truly transcend and move beyond every level by going through it, by integrating it, not by jumping over it. I first took the jumping classes, reached a very high level and then got bumped. This made me have to start at the first level again, properly. Just like a video game, you need to play and learn the level to be able to go further, you do not judge the first level as bad, it is just a first perspective of the game. It is vital that you build a strong foundation for transcendence, in the ground, in the material life, and that requires knowing how your instincts work, how your e-motions and sexual energy work, how your personal willpower works. And when you can infuse these with soul, with heart you get access to a whole lot bigger and more beautiful world than you ever imagined possible. You are then capable of relating to the magic and awe two thirds of the population still have access to, letting the best of both worlds unite and contribute to manifesting a whole different playing field.

## For eternity

The soul is our eternal part. It is the reason why people in India and Mexico celebrate the dead, for the soul enters a new phase of eternal life. I always intuitively knew that there was more to life than the way Western society prescribes and when my meditations got deeper, I got a taste of the reality beyond Western limits. It is magnificent. And at the same time it stretches you ever more in the beginning, it may even take away all of the firm ground underneath your feet. But that is just your view of life taking its new, truer shape. It may feel shaky at first, but paradoxically enough your ground is actually becoming stronger, it just needs some plowing first. Cardiologist Doctor Pim van Lommel and the neurosurgeon Doctor Eben Alexander use science to get a firmer grip on it, just like more and more Western scientists who research consciousness and the thing called death.

A couple of months after my first adult physical experience of coming into this world in the cycle of life-death-rebirth, I was confronted with the going out of this world. Twice, with only a couple of weeks in between. A dear friend of mine was taking care of a dear friend of hers that had leukemia, and although the cancer was gone, three of the young woman's vital organs had started to fail because of the chemo. The day before she died I asked my friend how she was doing. I noticed from her stories that everybody around the young woman had trouble letting her go, including my friend, so I advised her to allow her friend to gently leave for the next part of her journey. I knew the young woman needed help to be able to leave, as people often hold on to dying people making it hard for their souls to start the cross to the other side. My friend took the advice, with tears and a sad, but open heart. I learned that day that the young woman would soon be going as I got beautiful messages, like seeing a sign that said 'Angelo and the woman's surname'. I could sense a fantastic beautiful energy in the air, peaceful, gentle, sweet and soft. I could feel how the woman had fulfilled all she came here to live and learn, that she was truly ready to leave this life, even though she was only thirty-three. The energy I felt from her was deeply wise and gracious. The next day I received a message while still in bed. My first thought went to the woman, and I could feel how the energy field around her had completely changed. I understood she had crossed, for the sparkling was gone and the energy that I had always identified with her, was no longer there. She had evolved to another sphere. About twenty minutes later I received another message and jumped up to see if it might have been my friend needing help, but I had actually mistakenly received the message for my friend, who carries the same first name, saying the woman had passed away. The second one was to correct for the receiver. But I knew I got it not by mere accident. I am deeply grateful to the young woman for having showed me this experience of leaving in true grace and beauty, and all the Love that goes with it.

Only a couple of weeks later I had another experience from the other side. In winter I received a message that an acquaintance had been missing for more than a week in the mountains. I had known him for a short time, and it had been seven years since I had seen him. My reactions to his death were very intense, I could not understand why I was crying so intensely as I was at ease with death and only weeks before had supported that woman in crossing. I cried devastatingly and was pondering much on what could have happened. Strangely enough about a month before a woman had told me about how she had experienced her mother having had trouble crossing a year earlier, and her experience with it. Slowly I understood that his soul had come to me as his crossing was not going all that well either. I felt all his feelings, his deep fear, his anger, his confusion, his attachment to this life, his deep sadness for not having wanted it to turn out like that, and also his love. We communicated and I promised I would help him out, even though I had no clue yet of what to do, I said I would walk with him to the Source, no matter what, but I would do it from my living state, in our polar ways of life and death. So I played healing Indian songs and talked to him about the magnificence of the other side, of its ultimate beauty and love, on life and death, about how they are all the same, but just different in form and how it was time for him to remember the wondrous beauty of his soul. This whole experience stretched my worldview tremendously, as there is still a big difference in intuitively knowing and practice. Slowly, his emotions started to soften and his remembrance returned, by then he was giving me many gifts in return. He reflected his, and my, typical Western family pattern that held no consciousness or care for the sensitivity of the soul. It was in this time too that I read about how reincarnation had been forbidden in our region about two thousand years before, making us forget that separation lives within unity. At one point I could tell him that it was up to him to find his calling, as in that he would find his peace. But I also started to wonder whether I might have been part of his task, and I no longer knew who was actually helping who. When I had regained the tears that were mine, he was helping me on my journey to oneness of life and death, from his place in the spirit world. Just like the Native Americans have always said that we are guided by the spirit world. The moment of his crossing was Beauty beyond compare. I had read about people having a soul and a Soul, the first still part of your individuality and the second one where there is no individuality anymore, where it goes over into universal energy. I was able to feel how his soul gently and lovingly faded into its more essential form. I was blessed with a dear new friend who gave me the experience of all this love firsthand. I am forever in Love with him. And this is how I keep fulfilling my promise to remember him, with a big deeply touching smile.

These stories are likely very difficult to read if you have not yet had such experiences, but the reason I share them is to highlight the Western gap in dealing with life and death. More money is invested in keeping someone alive for another month, often at a quality level that is hardly worth living, than on dying gracefully or helping the young to live a gracious life. How extraordinary is it not of people in their last moments sharing how beautiful it is where they are going, showing serene surrender and offering deep comfort and wise lessons on life to the people staying behind? Only by knowing and understanding death, can we truly learn how to live, opposites always feed into each other.

# Passionate living

So I have lived the realm in between and have been shown where souls go into their higher Souls, but beyond that I have had only glimpses, beautiful glimpses of pure light and love. With every further development of mine, these realms may naturally open up further, as they are gifts for living with a true heart and open mind. It is what I feel brought peace to my soul. I am happy that I have lived this, as at twenty-five I already had the feeling of 'Is this it?'. Living in a linear society left me sad and, without deep fulfillment, my deepest soul yearnings left untouched.

To fulfill your being, to feel a deep satisfaction, you must feed your soul. Only peace lived from the soul, can make you experience everything with ease and reach a state of balanced emotions. Only when you are content and at peace with your spiritual journey, will you look naturally within instead of seeking fulfillment externally, which can be quite hard when you are not taught to listen to your soul. It can be hard when you were not taught how to align making a living with the true expression of your talents. When you are bombarded with material things to acquire, left without any heart filled food to help you hear your soul, you might easily live a lifestyle that is soulless and only focused on more and more of the same. But as the saying goes, you cannot expect a different result by doing more of the same. Material food is very different from soul food, you can have all the money in the world and still be unhappy, a fancy car will not keep your heart warm at night. So it goes with social contact, one soul friend feeds you more than ten superficial contacts can do. And when your soul yearns, it shows itself by depression. Depression hence is no stranger in Western society for no reason. Some six hundred years ago to be depressed meant 'to be in Saturn'. I liked the thought of Renaissance gardens often having a bower dedicated to Saturn, standing in a dark, shaded secluded place where a person could retire and enter the state of depression without disturbance. Depression is a consequence of feelings of self-worth being based upon certain qualities instead of the feelings themselves. It is a state that allows you time to clarify and develop the feeling consciousness that later in life will offer you great support. This state of being is beautifully related to the life-death-rebirth cycle. Depression and melancholy can be compared to the 'Bardo state', writes Thomas Moore insightfully, the state the 'Tibetan Book of the Dead' describes as the time in between incarnations, the time before the next birth into life. It is thus normal that you may feel you want to withdraw and not participate in life, as you are in between lives. And as there is no advantage in premature birth, the Bardo takes its time and when allowed, the wisdom and beauty gained appear.

When I was working at the university and management schools, I was truly passionate about my work. Working in the world of innovation is fascinating. I found myself at the source of progress and the betterment of humanity. Or so I thought, for I was very soon lacking something. Everybody was working on technological innovation, but I noticed that where we should have more time to ourselves with all these technological aids, we actually had less, so something was missing. I first researched trends and foresight, the managerial version of clairvoyance I came to realize, and then, as I had already taken the vision of sustainability with me from university, I dug into social innovation. Going ever deeper to get to the root of the theme, I came to the personal level. Organizations and societies are the sum of all its people. In my last job in academics I had the wonderful support of a very intelligent professor who was acquainted with the other realms too and we jointly realized that if I wanted to pursue my research themes of uncovering and supporting universal frames, in that moment, in that place, to hold high the essence of scientific research, I would have to leave that system and go on a discovery outside of it. To do my soul's work, I could only learn my lessons elsewhere. It took me several years to shake of the academic conditionings yet keep the good ones, as I was taught to always gather sources of both the pros and the cons and scientifically validate every detail, preferably supported by numbers, numbers that you could easily play with to get them working for you. But where did that leave my intuitive knowing then? So I researched intuition then and found a big discrepancy between the academic viewpoint and ancient old cultures. I opted for what I felt deep inside, at my level of consciousness then, was the closest to the Truth. It was the most liberating feeling when I could truly feel I did no longer have to find ways to adapt to a system that was more limited than my worldview and my life's experiences. Slowly allowing both to integrate set the best path. I allowed myself to follow my passion despite others' opinions, and now, every time I follow my intuition, I touch upon a state of peace, tranquility, love and bliss, that all is at one and at peace, that the divine is within me just as all mystical schools, or quantum sciences, teach you. You cannot reach that by intellectual behavior only. My intellectual ways had set me in the direction of wellbeing on all levels, but they had never told me that I get excited from creating a safe gentle haven for babies and people to grow into strong and joyful soulful men and women. So I jumped. With the thought in the back of my head that the worst thing that could happen, was that I would fall back on the ground. Which was actually a comforting thought, mother earth does indeed, always carry you.

# With open heart

When you are open to it, you receive many messages that

show you your path. My favorite choreographer Sidi Larbi Cherkaoui once said, 'I stopped dreaming. I approach reality now as fulfilled dreams.' When you start listening to your soul's voice, you might be brought to tears by how it supports you and guides you clearly. Yet it is your soul's voice, it is subtle, it does not shout. Only in the end when there are no other means left, when you are being extremely stubborn in not listening to your own core, it shouts via your body. It is your soul who gives you your direction and subtle information in life. First gently via your intuition and dreams, then via positive emotions, followed by negative ones and if you still do not listen to these words of your soul, you will become ill or break a leg so you have no other option anymore than to sit still and go within to contemplate for transformation. Positive messages are always there, but sometimes we just cannot see, turn a blind eye or forget about them. Our soul language is a genially built in system, refined yet strong. It will make sure your external distractions are stopped so it can be heard, as it is here for you for a reason. Just like your heart beating for you.

Unfortunately in patriarchal societies many have a closed heart due to defensive mechanisms or other protection modes against hardship. This takes you away from feeling your soul, from feeling whole as a person, from hearing the guidance of your innate heart intelligence. Your heart plays a crucial part in realizing joy and soul fulfillment. And you can only reach this with an open heart. An easy way to recognize your soul talking to you is to pay attention to what excites you the most, what gives you sheer joy? That is the engine to your higher self, to your soul. You can have extra support via the Vedic teachings, which use the mantra 'Yam' while meditating for activating the heart. If you say it within, you can observe what happens to you. You might bump into a numbed or hard wall at first, but there is definitely a beautiful garden behind it waiting for you. This is unquestionably easier to enter when you can laugh at yourself.

When you touch upon your heart and soul, your courage is strongly activated as your inner knowing knows the only true path for you to follow. If you can get on that path, you are aligned with everything, with the centre of the Universe and its power can easily move through you. It always flows through you, it is always there for you to tap into, but on your very unique path, it shows itself effortlessly, it is where you are in full power. It requires commitment to get on it and stay on it, as we were first taught differently. But it is just like going to the next grade and when you have the knack of it, you reach a state of effortless effort, where you can consciously see the Universe working for you. Here you live and stand in awe of the geniality of life. You can experience how its intelligence far supersedes yours and how you could never have dreamed it to be so wonderful! This only happens of course, when you are open, relaxed and make room for life's geniality to be shown and flow through you. I see it as trying not to walk my own way, but our aligned way, me and life together. Given my conditionings it was not always easy and I had to summon much courage and faith, but since I have touched upon the essence of the Universe, I know the law of love as the primordial law of life. Whatever we do, all has its value to guide us to that source of love again, to guide us to the true, authentic, empowered us. Life is about embodying our souls, where heaven and earth meet. With some guidance, truly every one's soul knows how to ignite and embody your knowing of the sacred science of love and holiness that unites you with the Universe again.

# Nature's food

Nature is a most powerful food, it has an intelligence that is so strong that it naturally rebalances itself. It may not do so in one human lifetime, but it will do so in her timeframe, on her conditions, which we as little organisms might not always like. But when you look closely and develop your consciousness so that you can tap into the wisdom of nature and the cosmos, just like ancient ways did and so called primitive tribes still do, you will notice that there is no mal-intent. Nature is of a higher consciousness than man, humans have to learn to vibrate again like they once did. It is like realigning your beliefs with the principles of nature. French behavioral professors have validated that employees whose window face on to trees and flowers instead of urban constructions, experience their job as much less stressful. And in product design, bio-mimicry, the art of developing products based on the principles of nature is taking off, as with eco-building and home grown vegetables do, all natural trends for rebalancing and bringing nature back into our daily lives. Nature is and will always be our non-stop teacher on how to live life, its mysteries, its power and its beauty.

## Pure consciousness

Focusing on masculine principles only made us loose many wise and powerful feminine principles throughout the centuries. And although it is late, it is never too late. To balance our world again, we need to join hands, the masculine and the feminine, modern knowledge and ancient wisdom, ancient knowledge and modern wisdom.

These days there are incredible physical and energetic technologies developed by very intelligent men and women that restore the balance, many of them based upon the intelligence of nature. Like mushrooms that eat plastic, of which we have created way too much, or energy grid monitoring systems and energy renewables for each individual house, or top-edge energetic healing modalities. There is so much good stuff happening.

The main thing in understanding your connection to nature is that the way you view the world and nature depends on your mind-state and whether you can switch in altered mind-states or not. The type and range of information you receive that forms your worldview is state-specific. Paul Devereux, a research fellow with the International Consciousness Research Laboratories group at Princeton University explains how Western consciousness is monophasic at this moment, which means that it is locked into one specific state of consciousness only. It thus has a very limited worldview. Nevertheless, the nature of our cultural environment and the results of our neurological processing, as this is the part in our brain responsible for arranging the information we receive, can be affected and developed into higher information processing capacity by meditation and the like. When you live monophasic you might wonder why people hug trees, but if you dare to open up, you might sense what they sense. When you hug a tree, rest on it or put your bare hands to it, you connect to its energetic field, a field that is full of negative ions and by touching it, these ions transfer to your energy system, revitalizing and balancing it.

When I was walking in Africa that day of the enchanted forest, I had started walking on my own with two dogs as I wanted to feel safe again in nature, restore my connection. I intuitively felt that having no recollection of how to feel safe in my own home, in Nature, affected me greatly. I realized how nature with a big N, is the higher version of nature with a small n, my nature. That moment of enchantment, of broadened consciousness was just magical. I felt as if I was in a fairy tale where all the plants and animals were my friends, the colours were deeper and all felt sweet and so alive. I felt as if I knew every tree, every stone and could hear the whispers of every bush. That is how man's connection to nature has naturally been, is written about in poetry, in legends and stories and can be yet again.

Nature consciousness is pure consciousness, it vibrates exactly in its own unique way, exactly as the way it was meant to vibrate. There are no mental detours or dead-end streets, it always follows its natural way. It is exactly like the difference between a maze and a labyrinth, in a maze you can get lost, but in a labyrinth you always get to the centre. Nature is like a labyrinth, where the lower human mind is often like a maze. But when you have spent much time in nature, you start resonating more with her and as such with your own unique nature. You evolve from a maze into a labyrinth and walk again into the essence that is your soul.

## Tuning in again

To vibrate with nature consciousness is something you can only learn by feeling into it. Ancient tribes developed their knowledge of nature and the animals by feeling into nature, they became nature, they became the plant or animal they were looking for. All was connected. Anthropologist Claude Lévi-Strauss found that they did not use logical systems to name and categorize their plants, as their wisdom was not based on such a consciousness, it was and still is much broader than that. There is a beautiful project in Australia named 'The Knowledge Initiative', that aims to collect aboriginal culture's wisdom and integrate it into higher education. It is highly valuable material. Their knowledge about water systems, plants systems, soil systems, all ecosystems are a necessity if we want to restore the balance of nature and our health again. This wisdom of nature, this animation, is being recognized more and more by the Western mindset, like many renowned international scientists such as Stephen Hawking having signed the Cambridge Declaration on Consciousness in Non-Human Animals on July 2012. Nature is wise.

To understand this and attain such nature wisdom, we must silence our minds first and foremost, the healthier your body, the easier to experience inner silence. When I landed back in Europe after my third visit to South-Africa, I instantly felt the disconnect of nature very strongly, I felt the pain, the lack of connection, as if it is engrained in our cultural genes. It only took three minutes before I felt a harness-like armor envelop my system, a non-feeling to nature to cover up the lack I became aware of. I could easily feel how Mary's roots in nature were once masterfully cut off and scandalized, and sometimes still are. Why forbid herbal medicine that comes free from our forests to all, why cut our forests that hold the balancing remedies for our ailments? Luckily there are still people that hold the balance. In its pure form, priests, and other wise men and women help you to go beyond this belief or feeling of separation. Priesthood is a deeply beautiful dedication, a beautiful contribution to people, as they are here to guide you to your own connection to nature again, the one with the small and the one with the big N, and the connection between them. They guide you to feel that God, the energy that animates nature, is within you, that you are never separated from universal power and love. In ancient Egypt there was even a priesthood of commerce, commerce was a way to reach enlightenment, a way to unite with your deepest essence and harmonize society. Imagine what qualities that would bring into our global economy if taken up again, imagine what that would do to the natural system and all the inhabitants on our earth.

As soon as you break through your armor, or walls or whatever other defense systems you have set up, you can reach that connection to nature again. When you resolve your fear, you will gain trust again, as fear from the mind indicates a lack of trust. Whereas learning to listen to the fear that comes from your belly, helps you gain safety. Once you go deeper and deeper within, you will experience that naturally. In the beginning you may only reach it when meditating safe in house, but after a while, you can practice true meditation, meditation in your daily practices and take your true nature out for a walk. 'I am' is the most essential meditation mantra. You learn to stay within when you are outside, you learn to act from within, where your masculine meets your feminine energy. From here, you grow your trust again that all flows in its divine way and timing. You just have to learn to listen and feel again.

Sitting in nature can help you with that. You start by listening to your thoughts, your emotions and your body and then you learn to listen to your heart, intuition and nature, more subtle forms of information. And after that you can learn to listen to the earth and cosmic energies. They portray higher developments of consciousness. In the beginning it may seem that they follow a sequence, but after a while you realize that they all operate simultaneously. At every step you slowly learn a new vocabulary to describe your experiences so you have a tool to communicate from within to without.

At one point when I meditated with a woman, she said to connect to the new earth, and when I did so, I felt a very different energy. It was not the earth in the way I had known her before. In this place, there was no room for dark energies to feed on themselves, it was a very gentle, fun and loving place. A friend of mine explained this beautifully, namely that nature is a consciousness related to a planet, genially indicating the global connectivity of our earth's body. And so, like earth, all planets have a nature, it is their consciousness that envelops an entire planetary system and together create the consciousness of our universe.

With epigenetics in mind, when you live in the city, you will vibrate more like the culture of the city. And when you live in nature, you will vibrate more in tune with the culture of the nature. Your actions will differ greatly, unless of course, you bring nature back into the cities. Northern Europe has really good city development planners, they kept much more of their natural cultural heritage when building roads and their cities. When they built their highways they even listened to their people that held their lore of elves and gnomes. They revere nature's spirits and the people who still feel into them. Their city planners do not keep their spiritual development for personal life only, they integrate it in the public domain as well. Some years ago when I was walking in Antwerp, my home town in Belgium, I had a vision of how nature had been brought back into the cities. The buildings were made of natural materials, plants grew against the facades and the air was so pristine. These visions of mine make me smile and give me much trust, this one clearly not being in such a distant future. Nature is finding its way back into our lives. Children that grow up in the cities will yet again know that their fruits and vegetables grow on trees, the walking people, as called by Native Americans, that make sure we can breathe healthily and keep our feet on firm ground.

# Cosmic food

When you are trained in meditation, in going deep within, you activate new levels of brainwaves and by that, new information. Every time you expand out into the universal field you can reach new levels and experiences, a bigger perspective on the world and life. Easily feeling you are an integrated part of it. It is magnificent how much nurturing you can find in these states, how much support and wisdom. You touch upon feelings that are deeply loving. You touch upon vibrations that are personified by Gods and Goddesses, archetypes from all cultures, yet lie within all of us waiting to be activated. In the West we have long forgotten about this food, although our ancestors had much knowledge and wisdom about these energies too. Besides practicing natural medicine, that is what our shamans did too, all mystics, yogis and naturally connected people still do, expanding out and activating their supra-sensory perception at will by meeting the profane with the sacral in intended contemplation, creating mystical experiences. This allows hyper communication, similarly to a queen ant who sends the building plans to her colony even from far away, known to us as inspiration or intuition, suddenly gaining access to information that is outside your own knowledge base. Yet, for successful hyper communication, for the information to be distinct and useful, stress, worries or a hyperactive intellect need to be out of the equation. So is it better to master a clear distinctive individuality merged with a collective consciousness, otherwise distortions rule the game. So, even if you were not brought up with it, or even taught to dismay it, your system will sooner or later recognize these places of contemplation and introspection that open doors to bright new worlds. You learn to trust the unknown and enter the world of quantum physics where a whole array of infinite possibilities unfolds.

## Left and right together

When you research Eastern and wisdom schools this is all very normal, tapping into cosmic energies are a part of daily life. You could say that cosmic food is something you can only eat when your right brain hemisphere is activated too. It is not accessible via the logical thinking all pervasive in the West, being the left brain's way. This is why many Western people cannot make sense of it, as it is only experienced, and so it is often feared and put aside as hocus-pocus. It is indeed a whole new world to be discovered and explored, but just like the left brain hemisphere has its own system of language and syntax, so has the right brain. It is just a matter of being trained to recognize and use it. You preferably use your left and right brain together, otherwise experiences may overwhelm you greatly. So even if you have been taught to suppress your right brain's capacities, by the religion of classic science or any other religion that you worshipped that did not stimulate your right brain qualities to be empowered, you can reactivate them again. Just like you can train your muscles back into shape after a period of no activity. Fortunately, it is not because culture has overwritten one of your instincts and abilities that you have lost them forever.

The qualities of the left brain hemisphere are masculine qualities and characteristics like analyzing, deductive reasoning, logic, specialization, quantifying, critical and systematic thinking with a common denominator of separation and duality. The qualities of the right brain hemisphere are feminine qualities and characteristics like synthesizing, inductive reasoning, intuition, integration, qualifying, nonjudgmental and empathic acting and thus feeling with a common denominator of connection and unity. So if you are trained to use your left brain only, there is no option for you to eat cosmic food, as it is a specialty of the right brain. Just like the quantum researcher could not grasp his findings with his left brain, by using his right brain, the part that knows no boundaries, he was capable of placing his new insights into the bigger picture, a quality that also comes from your right brain. The same goes with reading ancient texts, there is a big difference to interpreting them with your left brain, which reads it literally versus interpreting them with the right brain, which reads symbolically. If you consider on top of that in what holistic consciousness these texts were written, you get a very different interpretation of the stories all together.

For properly opening up and tapping into your right brain, you need your left brain qualities to evolve too. As a result, it is not one or the other, it is both you need. So education should not merely be learning facts, it should teach us how to use both brain hemispheres, ideally jointly. The internet stores all the knowledge these days, so you can train your brain much better for other things than mere storage and basic linking. If you know we only use about ten per cent of our brain, you have an opening to where to start looking to begin using more of it. It will definitely make you feel more whole with every new discovery. Your cells are waiting for you to use and connect all of them. But for sure you cannot just open up a whole new regiment without the proper support. The universe is big, the world is big, our bodies are big when you look at them from the level of how many cells and systems work together to make us function the way we do. Or do not anymore, depending on how well you have taken care of your system. As the saying goes, as above, so below. We can find the whole cosmos inside our bodies, we are undeniably a micro version of a bigger whole.

## Abundance

Much of our healing and new capacities lies in being a micro version of the cosmos. When, years ago, I did not find examples of women personalizing pure balanced feminine energy, I went looking for it on an energetic level. I closed my eyes and went into meditation. I had read about connecting to the universal energy as the masculine principle and the earth as the feminine principle. So I closed my eyes, became silent within and lovingly asked them to show themselves to me and teach me. And so they did. I was learning about the masculine and the feminine principle by my feeling consciousness. It was easy to recognize as your system knows, and it was astounding to observe the energies. They were pure loving energies, so powerful, so pure. They were each of a consciousness that was exactly balanced, no human ego involved that created one being better than the other. They just each were, beautifully themselves and distinctly different, and yet so exactly the same. You can also feel this difference in meditation and yoga styles. The feminine meditation and yoga style is about softness and surrender, it just follows whatever comes along, it is very diffuse and slow. It is about letting go, your senses, receptivity and spontaneity, it is about feminine fullness. The masculine meditation and yoga is about insight and wisdom, it focuses on one single point, is mobile and fast. It is about letting go, taking distance, about the masculine emptiness. Both very comforting and effective.

When you lacked some energetic examples in your life, you

can actually summon them via these. It is going from the law of attraction to the law of resonance. It is just a matter of raising your perception and frequency to a level that you can make the invisible visible, for we are after all a copy of the cosmos. If you lack faith in your life, you can meditate upon it, you sit still and evoke it. Of course you need practice, but at one point, if you are open, receptive and patient enough, you will feel the energy of faith, you can feel exactly what it does, how it behaves and what it does for you. If you listen closely, you can let it tell you what you need to change to bring more faith into your life. Even in the highly challenging case of domestic violence for example, if you dare to trust your heart's yearning for the feeling of knowing you are deeply loved, you can summon that love, feel it, get into your power and then act upon it. You can do that with everything, with beauty, with power, with peace, with wonder, with mother energy, with father energy, with joy, truly with everything. It is a beautiful source of food, a fridge so full, it never, ever empties. It is outstanding. And once you have filled your body with it, you will see how easily you will attract that faith or other energy in your life from then on. Meditation is a means to develop the capacity for a very strong loving heart, a heart that is capable of transforming sad things into happy things, fearful things into courageous things, heavy things into light things, ugly things into beautiful things, mastering the art of allowing something to die and be reborn in a higher form. It is fully active transformation. Similarly with meditative exercise like yoga, where you have a tree pose, a warrior pose, a pigeon or swan pose, all poses to strengthen our qualities, from the physical to the spiritual. Our surroundings are our mirror, as above, so below, as within, as without and tests will come and show you your skill and fortitude in managing an energy. The more open your heart, the more higher aspects can ground you into your embodiment, the more you can transform. You can enter these energetic places via indigenous ways, Eastern teachings or mystical traditions, they all teach access to the same cosmic energy.

## Exquisite heritage

In Native American lore, where the men go on vision quests, Jamie Sams shares how in her tradition the women are taught to connect to the thirteen phases of the moon, each standing for a specific aspect of truth. To learn the cycle of truth, we must learn, honour, know, see, hear, speak, love, serve, live, work, share and be thankful for the truth. With the thirteenth moon you learn to integrate them all. Sometimes it takes you on a road that on first sight seems to take you further away from your goal, but if you dare to follow it, you will see it genially brings you closer than you have ever been. Hence the importance of your moon time, your menstruation period. You can start to reconnect by sitting silently with the innermost part of you or look at the moon. You know the power of the moon, the ebb and flow it creates and, if you observe your surroundings during the full moon, you can notice many differences.

Hindu mythology knows many goddesses that all represent a part of feminine energy, all can be meditated upon to feel and feed yourself with the corresponding energy. So does meditating on yantras, sacred geometrical figures representing vibrations like beauty and peace that act as activation templates of consciousness. It takes practice, but the more open you are, the easier it becomes to feel the vibrations. There is also a millennia-old tradition of Durga, the Compassionate Mother and Fiercely Protective Female Warrior, also known as the Remover of Fear and Difficulty. According to myth, there are demonic forces trying to conquer the world destroying all who do not agree. In the myth the creator God Brahma made the demon king undefeatable by any man, god or demon. When the king was asked if he wanted to be excused from defeat by a female, he declined, as to his overblown ego, battling a woman was already won. He had not taken her power to emit a flame from her finger that would restore people to a state of tranquility and compassion into consideration. When the moment comes that Durga steps on the scene and takes on the battle to prevent the world from destruction, the demon king becomes ever more angry for his possible loss of control and power, losing himself and eventually losing the battle to Durga. This Goddess represents an energy of pure love and calmness that acts for harmony and unity. She personifies the energy of peace, healing, spiritual liberation and realization of inherent divinity for she is unconditionally loving, for anyone, ego demon or not.

In Buddhism when you enter ever further levels of consciousness, they speak about the higher powers. By this they mean psychological powers that are tapped into, powers that go with a more developed consciousness. These are qualities like seeing into the past and future, telepathy, healing so called incurable diseases and perceiving the so called invisible. Where Buddhism has always revered these higher powers, the Inquisition did the contrary and prescribed these to their purported witches. Whether you see this highly activated use of your senses as normal or paranormal, beneficial or maleficent just depends on the viewpoint you take and your own level of sensitization or desensitization. Buddhism sees it that the more loving you become, the more brain activity is created, the more powerful you will be. Because every time you grow in consciousness, it is because you have learned to accept more energies that make up part of life. Acceptance is hence crucial for transformation into higher levels, so is an open heart to stay grounded while in the higher planes. It is important to learn to give up your resistance to your own path, to yourself, even if they are tricky energies to learn to master. Despite how counterintuitive it may feel, your 'loving' obstacles are a way for you to grow more fully into the real you. When you are capable of accepting your current reality as your own creation and listen to its message, you can then grow profoundly, and you can then also destroy your own creations that do not fit anymore. For that your soul needs to be ready to face its hidden pains, accept them and then let them go. From there you can then create a higher reality. By having the absolute faith and trust that higher reality will be given to you and so be grateful for what already is that which is soon to be manifested, miracles will happen. In summary, it means you will have learned to balance countering energies, in its most essential form thus masculine and feminine energy. Imagine using these powers to address mundane complex tasks.

We have such extraordinary heritage about feminine energies in the West too, the remnants being the myths of the Greek goddesses that teach us which qualities to develop or heal to sooth our soul. But most of our feminine voices have been burnt, hidden, or have not yet found their way into the light again. Many ancient texts still lay in libraries waiting to reveal their secrets and while studying these, it has been uncovered that nuns had a large creative chair in the transmission of the sermons of their confessors, many sermons of priests were actually written down by nuns, in joined collaboration with other sisters and, or with the priests themselves. Despite history saying women were illiterate, nuns were literate in Latin too. A group of about hundred international scholars is dedicated to uncovering the voice of women in our history. We know some of them, like the abbess and mystic Hildegard Von Bingen, who reached a high status and the mystics Hadewych, Teresa of Avila and Beatrice of Nazareth but most women's voices and actions stayed within the confines of their convents. Nevertheless, we can trace their way back and forward.

# Receptivity

There is an energy field they call the 'Akasha', it is like the internet, a field that stores all information, all events, all feelings and thoughts, which holds all, but it is not manmade. In scientific circles it is researched by systems scientist Ervin Laszlo. When you learn to heighten your consciousness you can get access to this field. It requires a very refined energy though and it is not a level you can take or conquer. It is by observation and opening up that you are allowed to receive information from it. Giving is masculine energy, receiving is feminine in nature, just like our bodies unite in sexual love making. So you are to put your system into a receptive state to be able to perceive these higher states. Again, if you were taught to only give, like some old beliefs misinterpreted that you have to take care of others first, you will have to learn to receive again. In our patriarchal society there is often a negative connotation with receiving, hampering this natural process. You are to transform the belief that you are needy, poor or weak if receiving because you are worthy, and then you receive experiences from a whole other dimension. Women are naturally more endowed to receive, it is built in our system, but in the face of a patriarchal system, that mode of receptivity has often become quite tainted.

One of the ways to restore your receptivity is to develop

your intuition. All people are intuitive, it is yet another intelligence we can all use to our benefit. It is more developed in some than in others, it is like having a mind for math or an eye for art, but we can all tap into it whenever we want to and cultivate it. Intuition is the skill to pick up subtle information that is not directly perceived by one of the five senses, but by an invisible sixth sense. With training, intuition even becomes your principal organ of perception after a while. Intuitions are not something you look for, you just create space and they come to you. When your intuition is on, you have access to a greater creativity that is naturally out of the box. We experience intuition when we know something did not come from using our observation or linear or rational thinking processes, it is non-calculated non-local information gathering. You can compare it to experiencing beauty, it just is, there is no reasoning behind it. Unfortunately in most cultures the senses, just like our right brain training are not a subject for development in school, loosing us a great opportunity for the complementary education of a highly interesting and rewarding skill, not only for every individual but also for mankind. To be able to open up your intuition, it is essential to understand the fundamental differences between classic physics and quantum physics. The first one focuses on the weighty and the macroscopic and the other one on the subtle and the microscopic. They do not exclude one another. They study the same thing, but they just do not focus on the same level. It is wisdom that knows how to connect these two. It is very worthwhile to investigate the links between them, especially to understand our wellbeing better. Making room for true creativity in your life, and therefore transformation, requires that you address everything that influences you and how you view your reality. The less tainted you are by pains or cultural beliefs, the stronger your intuition will be, as the level of your intuition is mainly based upon the connection you have to your own body and heart. If you listen carefully whenever you need to make a decision in your life, you notice that your body produces a message of comfort or discomfort, showing you intuitively what direction to take.

When you start re-activating your intuition, it is important that you re-activate your inter-human boundaries, that you know how to separate yourself emotionally from your environment, as you will pick up much more information than before, not only about yourself but also about other people. This is why it is so important to develop your self-awareness and purify your individual and collective system, on the physical, emotional, mental and spiritual level. Energetic boundaries come into play then too, which take you a step further than human emotions. When you develop your intuition from scratch again, you can take it one step at a time. But when you were born with high intuition in a non-intuitive society, you can be quite tested. In South-Africa I met a beautiful young man who had visions in the future. Nice, you would say, but this twice involved someone close to him walking to their death. Although he was a big guy, it was easy to grasp his deeply sensitive nature. Since our society has lost its energetic understanding of the cycle of life-death-life, there is still a taboo on death, and so on the entire cycle, he was very afraid. I explained to him that his visions were actually a talent he was yet to learn to master and figure out how to use it constructively, that he was not to be afraid of death as there is no such thing in essence, only a change in form. Everything has two sides to master, sometimes very subtle, but in essence they are always manifestations of the basic duality of light and dark, night and day, waiting for the circle to be full. I like the metaphor that when sun and earth have lots of friction, light is created and when they have the same strength, darkness, the night is created. And we need light to grow. The recognition of his skill, instead of portraying him as mad or a psychic freak gave him more inner peace. And peace is an essential part of being successful, whatever your talent. The wise people in ancient and tribal cultures always knew how to deal with these energetic challenges, it was not seen as a figment of your imagination. It was the life that belonged to the invisible realms. The realms of the feminine principle that have an effect on our visible reality and we on theirs.

There is so much to learn about cosmic energies, it truly is a vast ground to explore. One time during a Vipassana retreat I was given the experience of celestial music. It was so beautiful, so pure. This cosmic world is there for you to feed yourself with deeply soul touching gifts that you may feed the world. Many composers hear their music in dreams like Mozart did, or hear it being played for them, and this is where their music comes from. Similarly with many scientists, who get their inspiration when they are totally relaxed, standing in the shower or resting in the garden, their inspiration coming from that same place. The Western world has tried to grasp intuition with the left brain, seeing it as a result of our unconscious. The East however sees it as a power of the higher mind, of the super conscious, it is called 'Buddhi' in their language, with the lower, rational mind called 'Manas'. They work very differently and you are to let each do the job it was designed to do. You need sensitivity to touch upon the power of the super consciousness though, it does not follow rational thinking, but heart thinking. It is soft and gentle, not hard and cold. The higher mind that connects you to your soul and higher spiritual, universal realms, cannot be grasped or experienced by the left brain, the left brain cannot reason its way into it. The left brain is exquisite, but instead of claiming domination over the entire world, it is there to live jointly with the right brain and the different levels of consciousness it can access. The right brain is capable of dreaming and journeying, and the left brain is capable of seeing how to manifest these dreams into reality. Together they would instantly create heaven on earth. In the end eating cosmic food is about you trusting your own inner voice, trusting what it tells you clearly, convincingly and without any doubt that a new world will manifest for you in daily life, where it connects you to heaven and earth. That is what kings and queens in the old days were precisely trained for.

# Tantric food

In tantra, the art of loving, everything comes together. Like Epifanus quoted earlier, tantric sexual union is not about a mere physical act, it is a physical union that is the earthy image of the divine oneness, here you unite heaven and earth. It is where masculine and feminine energies unite in their purest form, free of any limiting beliefs or cultural conditionings, so they create a consciousness well beyond each on its own. During an orgasm, 'the little death' as termed in French, when all your chakras are open and energy can freely rise from Shakti, when your base and feminine aspect unite with Shiva, your crown and masculine aspect, it is this unity consciousness that you touch upon. In conventional sex however, it lasts merely some seconds, if you are lucky, you can be there longer. When calculated based upon conventional sex standards you spend about fifty-five hours there in your entire life, I guess we all want more of that.

## Daring to love well

Our bodies help us to find, or refind, true love, every time with a more refined current, a deeper, truly free one without an invisible unconscious undercurrent. Tantra lets us move. It is about emotional maturity, about purifying your animal instinct and surpassing your sexual instinct and sacred unity, it is a life art to live life fully. It transforms regular lovers into deeply revered lovers, it helps women and men to heal, to open up to life, completely, not merely physically but deeply energetically too, in bed and in daily life. Tantra is wondrous, it can even transform the world as the focus shifts from I to we. And as a woman it will surely transform the way you relate to men, and to yourself. So start by asking yourself, 'Do I love well?'.

Because of betrayal and disappointment, by trauma of individual experiences or from the collective image of womanhood that we carry in our genes, many women end up having their body and heart closed down. From being joyfully alive, it is like becoming dead inside and longing deeply to be reborn. When life makes you touch upon that deeply hidden image of a betrayed womanhood via your intimate relationships, it is indicating you are ready and strong enough to move beyond it into a womanhood and masculinity from where you can and know how to deeply trust. For that, it is vital that you become aware of how you bonded and lived your sexual energy in the past, so that you are able to make conscious choices in the present moment. In which sexual experiences was your heart in it, and in which ones not, even at moments in long relationships? Did you maybe suppress your sexual energy and have only asexual surrogate relationships? Did you maybe practice 'brahmacharya', the yogi practice of celibacy to experience no sexual desire so that you could use your sexual energy for personal and spiritual development bringing you phenomenal spiritual experiences, yet getting out of touch with the physical? Or on the contrary, maybe you got so desensitized that you publicly presented yourself in a sexually harsh or easy way, leaving no room for sensuous private sexual intimacy? Did your choices come from within, or from something you read in a magazine or saw on TV? In all, along the way, which discoveries did you like, which ones opened you up and which ones did not at all fit you, making you close down? Which is your unique form of sexuality that opens up both your genitals and your heart? With whom and how do you connect to people in general? To what do you connect? Do your contacts speak for love, passion, for pleasing energy, your unhealthy ego, your wound or out of a misunderstanding of love? Is there equality in your relationships, or does one silently fancy the other or subjugate the other? And above all, is there mutual trust? Only by becoming aware of it can you consciously choose how to enter a new or renewed relationship with someone, whether intimate or not. Are you ready to let go of a lifestyle and relationships that had you circulating on old levels of development, keeping you small and hampering your next evolutionary step? Do you know what it is you truly want? Are your old ways and relationships supporting and adding to your dream life vibration and expression of it or not?

As Western men and women we are rarely taught about the art of life. Sexual energy is our life energy, our creative energy and is meant for that, to create, not to react. When you learn to use your sexual energy creatively in your own unique way in a sexual relationship, free from conditioned undercurrents, you are set to use your creative expression in any domain of life. To freely flow, you are able to express yourself sexually without being judged or judge upon. Western women are rarely taught how to fulfill their deepest needs and satisfy their deepest longings, they are rarely taught how to deal with their sexuality nor the art of deep intimate relationship, communication and healing skills. On the contrary, they are mainly taught to tune into an unbalanced version where women sell themselves naked on every corner of our streets. This is why so many women are still not satisfied sexually nor with their lives, with all consequences for herself, her relationship, her family and society. Moreover, countless women have these old programs running that sex is a duty, or that women are property who have no right to enjoy pleasure or the creative force of the essential energy flow of life. A long time ago however, there were temples where priestesses helped you to be open and learn to sustain sacred relationships, where earthy and cosmic energies unite. In those days women knew about their contribution to society via practicing sacred sexuality, they knew about lust, sexual desire, being equal to the lust for life and celebrating life, they knew how to naturally uncover it and how to live it honourably. They knew their high value and joy in being a woman and sharing that with their man. This knowledge of how to use your sexual energy in a sacred way got pushed aside, and for many women only very little or the backside of it was available with its strongest potential staying hidden.

The marketing agency of Just Ask A Woman found that in advertising about eighty percent of the ads for women are created by men, fantasizing men, who clearly are very rarely sexy sensual tantrics and got stuck somewhere at the sexual age of an adolescent stuck in an old era. I wonder what the advertising and media world would have looked like in a matriarchal culture, and how it would have influenced the average definition people hold of 'sexy'. Unhealthy imagery of women, femininity and gender inequality starts already in G-rated movies for children, media created by grown-ups for children. Research done by The Geena Davis Institute on Gender in Media showed that for every one female character there were three male characters, in a group scene it changed to five male to one female. The majority of the females were highly stereotyped and, or hypersexualized, never the males. Sexually revealing clothes were the same in G-rated movies as in R-rated movies. And practically the only aspiration female characters had was finding romance, whereas hardly any male character had such a goal. And on top of that, in animated movies females had body types that could not exist in real life. Her institute successfully works on educating the media and the entertainment industry and supporting them in finding and delivering healthy ways to communicate to our children. Is it not wonderful to see the number of animated heroine-movies having scored big time since 2014? So, the work of the San Diego-based Centre for the Study of Women in Television and Film who found only eleven percent of the protagonists in the top 100 US films in 2011 were female characters, is paying off. Similarly, to create awareness on the topic, some Swedish cinemas have introduced a new rating called 'the Bechdel-test'. To get an A-rating a movie should count at least two named actresses, and talk about something else than a man. The goal of the test is not about the movie's quality, but to show more feminine stories and perspectives, since our view on the role of women in society is influenced by the roles of women on the big screen. The Annenberg Public Policy Centre at the University of Pennsylvania showed that female characters were twice as likely to be seen in explicit sexual scenes as males, while male characters were more likely to be seen as violent. Let us not forget how male characters are portrayed either, they too have to look hard to find a noble role model. All these organizations highlight and advocate a transformation in our inner play of dominance and submission active within all of us, our heart and our yoni were taught to be in battle, not in balance. What was the media's message now, whole beauty or whore beauty? When women feel ashamed or not worthy of being a passionate woman with desires and needs, when teenage girls are called a whore for having a sexual experience by jealous girls, when sexually initiating women are seen as whores in a community where sex is the devil's doing or for having a baby before marriage, or for turning a man down or highlighting his sexual incompetence or lack of honour, respect and dignity, and where sexually exciting words for women are used that are words of insult in another context, or naked boobs that are longed for in media but should not be shown in the slightest while breastfeeding a baby publicly, their sexual and creative power are scandalized too often. Women carry this in their genes and it requires deep transformation. Notice how closely the words whore and whole are related, just like the words hard and heart.

When I consciously touched upon this, practically global, cultural energy pattern, everything changed. It reminded me of the unfortunately silliest thick book in my library, which is a book called 'Never marry a woman with big feet'. It is about women in proverbs over different cultures and over different times, it was very sad and shocking to see how demeaning language has been for women, how men were warned on the dangers of women. And the more alive the woman, the more beautiful the woman, the more dangerous she was perceived. It is a judgment and a prejudice that is well carried in our unconscious, by men and women. To learn to stand in your full womanhood, keep your ground and stay strong, you are likely to learn to deal with demeaning language. When people try to diminish your light, it is because your bright light illuminates their lack, impotence, or non-existent choice or focus to live their shining core, simultaneously testing your spirit. When you walk this path and take the lessons, one day or another you reach a tipping point, where what once made you feel uncertain or ugly, then makes you feel ever more secure and beautiful and helps you radiate ever stronger in your true identity, making you no longer a victim of others' behavior. On the contrary, you can use their behavior to strengthen yourself. When you own who you are and no longer give your light away, as, in the end, it shines for you first and foremost, you can show others what it is like to shine one's true colours. At times it might be a harsh lesson to learn but when you come to understand that everything has its shadow and its light side, including the path of beauty, the path of aliveness and the path of identity, you have reached a new level of mastership. To fully learn something, both sides, both schools are necessary and equally important to be able to play with.

The consequence of this old wound of betrayed feminine aliveness is that in Western society quite a lot of women have learned how to use their sexual energy to attract a man very well, but from its shadow, not in its pure form, making the old proverbs a reality, to the disadvantage of all women and men. In Western society quite a lot of men and women play on the instinctual level of sex, like the women literally creating a baby with a man without his consent, by playing on his weakness or abusing her strength. With that play of unhealthy dominance and submission active in a relationship, the overall satisfaction is very poor, and of no lasting nature. When your love and passion are fighting, having no balance between them, there is no capacity for enduring fulfilling relationships. The deepest longings of both men and women, that are an innate part of everyone's heart, cannot then be answered. Both women and men are often seen as merely a toy that you can use to fill your unconscious hollowness. The sexual experience is reduced to a merely bodily experience, and when played out, the search starts for another body. The story and hunt for fulfillment will remain the same though, until true love comes into play and the instinctual level can be transcended. When you come to understand that you can use your sexual energy in different ways and on different levels, you can consciously choose how to connect your sexual energy with another. And conscious choices make it a whole other game.

When women chose to use their sexual, creative energy for abusing, instead of using their sexual attractiveness to get men attached to them, for money, a baby or to not be alone, it is only normal that a hostile environment takes shape. We have to be honest about the ways women go to war too, against men, and against women. We have to be honest how women sometimes forget how to support their sisterhood and brotherhood. Quite some women abuse their power for union, some unconsciously, some consciously, since they were taught to use it this way. So do quite some men. But to unite deeply together, truly, intimacy and vulnerability are required, from both sides. But vulnerability is still seen as a weakness instead of strength. Understandable of course, when given that vulnerability was not treated and honoured in the way it deserved to be. When you want to enjoy true union, there is no room for defensiveness, ego games, superior and inferior positions, labels, manipulation, control, false convictions, begging or taking seduction for love. Nevertheless, these are what women, and men, are often taught to apply in the intimacy play. Nothing is said about intimacy itself, which requires the capacity to merge into one and to be separate, to come together and be alone, or about surrendering to yourself and another, about openness, abundance and innate bodily intelligence, or being authentically sexy from deep within and seducing so as to play with passion and love, when these are actually the ones that offer you deep pleasure and fulfillment in relationships. Leading and following from the heart creates such a different game.

# Uniting poles

To lead and follow soulfully, both man and woman must surrender to their own nature, to their true identity.

Only then can they offer their own quality fully to one another, and get to where total unity happens. Only in this surrender to ourselves and one another, can we feel completely safe as nothing needs to be kept hidden anymore. Conventional sex is mostly about sensation and tension, both masculine principles, tantra however, is about sensitivity and relaxation, it is about relaxed arousal, where both principles unite naturally. The union of subtle energies can only happen in relaxed surroundings. Which means that the man has to be able to use his sexual energy in a relaxed way, no tension to stimulate or hold an erection are part of this play. You can imagine then that it requires quite a mastered mind, heart and body in a man to be able to do this. Quite some have to broaden their scope and mature sexually to practice tantra. For a woman, it requires feeling emotionally safe and free and being ok with letting go of control over your desires and self-control. Neurologically translated by Glenn Wilson and Chris McLaughlin in 'The science of love', it is allowing your brain parts responsible for moral convictions and social judgments to become paralyzed, even better, cleansed. Hence the importance of setting yourself free from your cultural collective unconsciousness and just let your body talk. If you both can allow your body wisdom to move for you again, a wisdom untainted by cultural, religious or social conditionings, you are in for ecstasy. The more ecstasy, the deeper the peace, the communion and happiness within. That is what the transformational power of the story of Mary Magdalene, of divine roots in nature, of inner development is really all about. Underneath it all, lies a deep inner harmony, a bliss, waiting to be uncovered and revealed, just like blowing dust from a beautiful painting.

The Western sexual conditioning is based upon a dualistic consciousness that has forgotten how to move into union and reconciliation, whereas tantric sex is about a unity consciousness, it is about uniting poles. So it is very important that women contribute their natural energy to the play too. When a woman goes deep within, when her heart, body and soul are deeply fed, her uterus actually produces waves that generate a very special, and deeply spiritual energy that the man may receive via her. But this requires making love and playing with energy, it is not just about doing mere sexual positions and release of a built-up tension. Tantra is about going away from your head or genitals into your entire body, heart and soul, it requires activating your feeling consciousness by both man and woman. When you unite deeply, woman becomes man and man becomes woman. A woman connects to and activates the inner feminine energy part of the man and the man connects to and activates the inner masculine energy of the woman. You become bigger than the giving and receiving and move to the next level where you share, where you become greater than the sum of both. It is a wondrous way to learn to be whole within yourself and together. Also physically, as you step into your own healing modalities. With sexual play vital energy is released which nourishes and detoxes your organs and cleanses your senses, after all sex is a joining together of our sensing bodies.

For this vital energy to be released however, you need to unite your poles. Women have their positive pole in their heart and their negative pole in their genitals. With men it is the opposite, their positive pole is in their genitals and their negative one in their heart. To be a deeply happy human being, you want to restore the natural sexual current between your heart and your genitals, the true relational power of sexuality. A happy heart in an open happy body. So to generate electricity you want to activate each positive pole first, without tension. For a woman this is why sphere, her breasts and nipples are so important and for a man his penis. And since we both have an innate intelligence, the quality of the touch makes or breaks it all, deep tenderness needs to be in it from the start to be able to open up safely and fully so that other energies can come into play. When a woman's positive pole is activated her negative pole is naturally activated too and gets ready to receive her man. When she does not feel loved or cherished however, there will be no activity, no vividness. The connection between a woman her heart and yoni is very strong. Similarly, being afraid or with an unconscious conviction of being forbidden to express yourself sexually or enjoy sex, many women anesthetize themselves to inner bodily pleasure. This suppressed feeling consciousness however should not be confused with a woman who does not feel a man's masculine energy and self-love because they are too weak, although it tells the same story. So many women have put up major boundaries disliking their wounds, rejecting their magnitude, and so not loving themselves at all, making it impossible to surrender. For opening in sex and love, you are to open to yourself first, opening your heart for the depth of the true you and let your boundaries down, let your deep sensitivity and sensuality get back in, gradually, to become a strong woman again who can feed into her own and a man's body, heart and soul. When we are completely open and loving, you make love, see and treat your man like him being the most exquisite version of himself, and you feel he sees and treats you like the goddess you are, you sense that you see the other and yourself through your souls. In tantra this is called transfiguration, we apply it naturally when in a loving state. It is seeing beyond what is apparent, it is about inviting the reality that transcends appearances, in a dimension that is closer to the truth, closer to the core of the person. And since your souls recognize the quality, you will slowly start resonating with it and the image you made through transfiguration will become your new reality.

# Opening up fully

To open up fully in love making, a sexual connection needs to be set up in two steps, the foreplay and the actual meeting of one another. Foreplay serves as a means to let both partners enter into a resonant vibration, which drives them progressively to that feeling of becoming one. It serves to let boundaries come down and surrender to one another. Here you find the importance of healthy bonding again, whether you developed your self-consciousness, your identity well or not. If it was hurt and you are afraid, it will be very difficult, if not impossible to let go of your boundaries and enter that sacred space of unity. But if you build or rebuild your own sense of self, then everything becomes possible again.

The second stage is what the Taoists see as an alchemical process, a mutation and a transformation. Where in the first part it is a matter of moving within a known dimension, the second part throws you into the unknown, the mystery, into creation itself, remodeling your structures and enlarging your consciousness. Energy waves flow through your bodies, unite them and adapt them through the contact of your bodily fluids. The central organ or the place that corresponds to this all is the uterus. Taoists call it the 'alchemical cauldron' or the 'resonating case', as this is the place where the sexual energies, the life energies of man and woman come together, and through resonance are amplified and unite into an orgasm, it literally works the energies and gives them back transformed. Both partners feed into this cauldron, the woman by opening more and more space inside her and the man by investing in it, being nourished in return. For sure this requires sexual education or a talent on both sides. Saida Désilets, a young vibrant woman, developed a method based on

Taoist teachings specifically for women, on how to work your sexual energy or regain your sexual innocence. Her work is very important, since how many women are there who have shut their presence down, or feel afraid of a man penetrating them? Hence, a man is to be taught at his end how to enter a woman with trust, confidence and loving power in order to truly exchange energies with her.

Besides an active lifestyle, as we know and find normal in the West, it is thus essential for both man and woman that you keep contact with your still point, with your heart and soul, and retreat and relax amply. In bed the same rules apply on how to live life in a balanced, healthy and fulfilling way. Activity alone can actually create madness or depression. Which brings us to porn. When you start living tantra, porn can truly make you cry. The subtle may lead to the raw, whereas the raw does not so easily lead to the subtle, they cater for different things. Porn creates much tension and has no connection to the heart which makes it a very hard interchange of energy, portraying a specific way how men and women treat each other. If you think life and life's energy is only about being active, to achieve, be ambitious or conquer, you are only seeing one side of the coin, the unbalanced masculine version. To live fully and deeply fulfilled, you need a balance between activity and stillness. Just as you use your right and your left leg to walk strongly, while you actively raise the right your left is waiting, in active stillness, helping on earth. Here lies a deep insight into natural leadership. Natural leadership is given, it has moved beyond the level of dominance. When a man lets his woman be on top, consciously gives her the lead, vulnerably surrenders to her guidance, while she has evolved enough to not be seduced to dominate anymore, it is tremendously empowering for both. So is it when as a woman you surrender to the natural leadership of your man, it is like the best melting on the planet.

Tantra love making is sometimes mistakenly believed to be always gently loving. Women are honestly much more than that. In Hindu you have two Goddesses Lakshmi and Kali who you can compare to our Mother Mary and Mary Magdalene. Lakshmi represents the gentle and soft and Kali the fierce aspect of the feminine. A common conviction to set straight is that it is not that you are either sweet or a bitch, that would be too easy to describe the complexity and magnificence of being a woman. It means that you are standing in another aspect of being a woman, very strong aspects. Kali takes a lead role in tantra, for she is often seen as the highest reality of all deities. She is the Goddess of empowerment and is also associated with death and destruction, and seen as the slayer of demons. When you reach a state of unity, of bliss while love making, this is the place where death is transcended. With further learning, you can even feel the energy of death, and it is strangely enough for us Westerners, deeply sweet. That is how powerful this feminine energy is. It brings you back to your original state.

## Sharing in love

So to create the energetic circle between a man and a woman, it is very important for women to love their true selves, a very hard job in a patriarchal society. When a man enters a woman with love, truly respecting her unique nature, focusing on her heart, she automatically radiates her love and energy to his heart, opening it up which strengthens his positive pole and completes the circle. That is why it is essential for men to develop their feeling consciousness too, to truly unite for love, not for mere bodily gratification.

In that way, men themselves are responsible for the way women feed them with their energy and make them feel whole or not. Men have a tremendous power that should be nurtured and taught, it is of a primordial essence. Allowing yourself to be carried by a man, is deeply activating your feminine nature. The 'yam-yum position' in tantra shows that best. In this position your man sits in lotus position and you can allow yourself to fall gently in his lap. The deeper you can release your conditioned independence as a woman, the deeper you can surrender energetically to be carried by his body, energy and love, the deeper your trust and strength grows. In allowing this dependence, true independence as a woman naturally unfolds.

This all is also why women have to be careful about sleeping around and casual sex without love, something many so-called independent women do. You can do it, but you have to love it truly, otherwise it is harmful to your very essence. For it to be healthy your heart needs to be in it too as that is your positive pole, only then can it feed you. When you receive the energy of a man, as that is what a woman does, she receives, you must be aware that you have to digest that energy too, it becomes part of you and you will radiate it back into the world. If you sleep with men that are unfulfilled and sleep with women as if it were a sport, you are denying yourself the true sexual food your system needs to thrive. When a man feeds you with you being an instrument to his bodily gratification, be conscious of what food he gives you, and you give to yourself. You might think you are not worthy of more than that, but if you practice with your own feminine energy, you will come to see how worthy and powerful you actually are. Even if you fall back every now and then, try to move beyond your linear point of view, and take every step as a win. So it is important to use your own masculine energy and set your boundaries, be aware of making love to emotional, compulsive and egoistic penises that do not know how to be lovingly present and radiate true interest inside of your belly. A man's mother issues do translate into women issues. If a man could get a glimpse of the difference between an orgasm via Western conditioning or via the tantric way by his own doing, he would quickly be fascinated and change his ways. So would you. He would soon realize that your fulfillment is his fulfillment too. A tantric man knows that the level of his fulfillment comes from the level of your fulfillment. And when you both reach that state of being love, you naturally give and receive more and more love. Then you master the essence of the game and have come to understand your transformational power.

The man, or men you attract in your life are the living mirror of your inner masculinity and they will treat your femininity in the way you belief it is worthy of. If you have men that do not honour you like you need, you will have to look for the solution deep within yourself and restore your own protective powers. It will be time then to change your conditioned weaknesses into inner power. When you work with your femininity, your masculinity will get refreshed along the way and vice versa. Realizing that insecurity over your feminine powers feeds the ego and allows domination, helps you to understand that such events are but invitations to become secure with the true woman that you are. Realizing that uncertainty is a way to help you to live from deeper within, you open a door to trusting your inner being again. When you allow the realm of uncertainty, you actually allow the universe to work out the details for you. Realizing that vulnerability is a strength that makes openness possible and all the experiences this state allows, makes it attractive again. Being vulnerable actually requires strength. In a relationship, when you start tantra, you can expect your body to open and show all the emotions and tensions it has held. It is important you both support this process, all the way through difficult moments when things come up that you have carefully tried to hide your entire life. The power of a man's penis can actually heal a woman from all her pain, individual and collective by making love to her deeply, over and over again. A man who is consciously healing himself, a man with an open heart, who is integrating his inner feminine with his inner masculine can actually reverse the disease of disaffection that has set itself deeply in the tissue of a woman's belly. It is like uploading new information, being given true consideration and love. Imagine what can happen when you are fully loved. Men hold a magnificent power, often still dormant but waiting to be activated. A man can open a woman, support her in letting go of old wounds and consciousness levels, letting her go in the process and letting life's energy move through her. And as it goes, letting go takes love. Here lies true masculine power, a supportive, nurturing and strong masculinity. In return he receives the most beautiful woman deeply feeding his manhood. And so too, can a woman reignite a man's body, heart and soul. We are both powerful creatures.

## Making rainbows, a way of lovemaking

Huna, the ancient spirituality practiced in Hawaii has always had a system of learning how to make love, their approach to love making is truly beautiful, right up until conception. Huna specialist Rima Morrell writes that they make an explicit connection between making love and making, increasing consciousness, or making rainbows. Huna sees sex as sacred, and so knows a very different social conditioning. Young Polynesian boys receive a subincision for example, a longitudinal cut in the foreskin to increase sexual pleasure. This is contrary to circumcision which makes the penis less sensitive and decreases pleasure, with the intent of being focused less on the earthy, and more on God. Since in Huna it is all about sacred sex, subincision is not just about mere physical gratification, on the contrary. The operation holds deep symbolism and is intended to cancel the power of the subconscious, of emotional dangers, to increase the 'mana', or universal power. Older Polynesian children are taught how to make love the conscious way and enjoy themselves sexually, contrary to the West where we are left to mostly learn on the job. How beautiful is it, that in Hawaiian vagina, "amo hulu' is translated as 'esteemed sparkle'. On a deeper level, consciousness, force and substance are taught as essential aspects for effective love magic. And for that to stay alive, one needs to keep on growing, be prepared to let go by taking true responsibility, self-mastery versus controlling others. So before experiencing the result of their work and enjoying love making, much inner preparation and growth is required. A partner is chosen with whom it feels right, with whom you can regain consciousness, with whom you can align your three minds, subconscious, conscious and higher conscious. All requiring sincerity, true hearts and refined perception. Being in love and loving is not the same in Huna, in the first you only see what you want to see but the second is open and eternal, that is the true path. Sacred sex is vital for Huna, which teaches that life begins at the moment of conception, called 'the first glimmer of moonlight', with a child coming from the shared dream of a couple. Therefore orgasm is given revered attention, as it is 'a way of breaking through to the land of the gods', parents know the importance of directing their consciousness and allowing for something bigger in life. The ultimate form is the cosmic orgasm, where you are no longer aware of your body and your consciousness opens fully.

I have been blessed in experiencing that, I then came to feel broken, lost my trust and capacity to deeply connect and built giant steel gates around my heart. However I kept walking to once love relaxed again and restored and refound myself refined. Honouring, enjoying and loving my nature is yet again part of my life, more subtle, deeper, conscious and stronger than ever. From a tough femininity, through a vulnerable femininity, into a strong femininity that dances joyously with her masculinity. I have learned to bring my shadow home into my light.

When we choose to live in the land of rainbows, where a woman activates her masculine side to manifest her feminine energy into this world, giving voice to the bodily, energetic and cosmic energies in the private and public arena, you get truly powerful and beautiful women. What you can dream, you can realize. In that land of rainbows where a man activates his feminine side, his qualities of trust, beauty and care together with his masculine energies, you get truly powerful and handsome men. When you transform the one-sided masculine living of unbridled activity, power and possession and make space and time for wonder so as to reach silence, and be open for sincere friendship, stewardship and love again, you can create a very different society and set an example for the ones you love, big and small. What you can dream, you can realize. Imagine a world where a culture reigns where women and men share a relationship that is whole, inside and outside, where one feeds the other, helps to strengthen their wings and roots so that it becomes possible again to create heaven on earth. Imagine the power that is released and available when masculine and feminine energies again find their natural balance. There lies true happiness, true beauty, love, courage, faith and power, there lies heaven on earth.

Imagine yourself as being whole, being fully the woman that you are, your divine self manifested on earth. I hope you have received my invitation to be you, the balanced, true version of yourself, I would be honoured to meet her one day.

*You always had the Power my dear,*
*you just had to learn it for yourself.*

Glenda from the Wizard of Oz

# Bibliography

**Quotes from** Ph.D. and Author Marilee Adams, Neuroanatomist Doctor Jill Bolte Taylor, Doctor Tim Brieske of the Chopra Centre, Doctor psychiatrist Olivier Chambon, Doctors and Authors Deepak Chopra and Rudy Tanzi, Author David Deida, Author Epifanus, Chair at the California Institute of Integral Studies and Advisor to the UN organization Religions for Peace Jorge Ferrer, Hippocrates, Cancer specialist Doctor Josef Issels, Emeritus Professor Daniel Kahneman, Choreographer Sidi Larbi Cherkaoui, Astronaut Edgar Mitchell, Professor Morton Smith of the University of Colombia, Trainer and Speaker Christian Pankhurst, Plato, Lakshmi Puri from UN Women, Author and Entrepreneur Ayman Sawaf, Philosopher Arthur Schopenhauer, Researcher and Author Ihsa Schwaller de Lubicz, Scientist Carlo Ventura, Teacher and Author Marianne Williamson

**Research from** Neurosurgeon Doctor Eben Alexander, Teacher and Author Laura Amazzone, The Annenberg Public Policy Centre at the University of Pennsylvania, Cranio-Sacral Therapist and Author Marijke Baken, M.D. Jean Shinode Bolen, The Centre for the Study of Women in Television and Film, Psychotherapist Catherine Crawford, Neuroscientist and Professor Richard Davidson at the University of Wisconsin-Madison, Entrepreneur and Author Saïda Désilets, Research fellow International Consciousness Research Laboratories Group Paul Devereux at Princeton University, Author and Speaker Wayne Dyer, Doctor Riane Eisler of The Centre for Partnership Studies, Doctor Masuru Emoto, The Environmental Toxicology Program of the National Institute of Environmental Health Sciences in the US, Neurologist and Professor Cordelia Fine at University of Melbourne, Documentary Forks over Knives, The Geena Davis Institute on Gender in Media, Heart Math Institute, Institut de Recherche sur les Expériences Extraordinaires INREES magazine, The Institute Reinier De Graaf, Marketing agency Just Ask A Woman, Professor of Psychology Dacher Keltner at Berkeley University of California, Journalist and Author Guido Kindt, Systems scientist and founder of the Club of Budapest Ervin Laszlo, Anthropologist Claude Lévi-Strauss, Researchers Lilly and co, Doctor Bruce Lipton, Author Walter Makichen, Care Expert and Health Writer Chris

McLaughlin, Massachusetts Institute of Technology MIT Journal, Ph.D. and Author Thomas Moore, Fellow of the Royal Geographic Society and the Royal Anthropological Institute Ph.D. Rima A. Morrell, Writers Claire Nahmad and Margaret Bailey, Coach and Author Riet Okken, Researchers Olsson and co, Doctor Candace Pert, Teacher and Author Diana Richardson, Researchers Romieu and co, Neurologists Rubenstein and Merzenich, Native American Wisdom Author Jamie Sams, Entrepreneur and Author Ayman Sawaf, Professor Doctor Emeritus Mineke Schipper, Sensi©-plan, Traditional Knowledge Initiative, Cardiologist Doctor Pim van Lommel, Emancipator and Author Lutgart Van Parijs, Professor in Business Ethics Thomas White at the Loyola Marymount University, Phsychologist Glenn Wilson, Neuroscientist and Professor Sandra Witelson at the McGil University, Women's Health Initiative and Ancient Egyptian, Buddhist, Christian, Native American, Sufi, Tantric, Taoist, Vedic and Yogic teachings

*May*

*peace*

*be*

*in*

.

*your*

*heart*

Printed in Great Britain
by Amazon

80936755R00121